Levels 3–6

BREAKTHROUGH
READING

David Grant
Julia Hubbard
Sarah Donnelly
Consultant: Cindy Torn

www.heinemann.co.uk
✓ Free online support
✓ Useful weblinks
✓ 24 hour online ordering

0845 630 44 44

Heinemann

Part of Pearson

Heinemann is an imprint of Pearson Education Limited, a company incorporated in England and Wales, having its registered office at Edinburgh Gate, Harlow, Essex, CM20 2JE. Registered company number: 872828

www.heinemann.co.uk

Heinemann is a registered trademark of Pearson Education Limited

Text © Pearson Education Limited 2009

First published 2009

13 12 11 10 09
10 9 8 7 6 5 4 3 2 1

British Library Cataloguing in Publication Data
A catalogue record for this book is available from the British Library.

ISBN 978 0 435806 22 4

Designed and produced by Wooden Ark
Original illustrations © Pearson Education 2009
Illustrated by Tony Forbes, Rory Walker, Paul McCaffrey, Kathryn Baker
Cover design by Wooden Ark
Picture research by Zooid Pictures
Cover photo/illustration © Getty Images
Printed in the United Kingdom by Scotprint

Acknowledgements
The author and publisher would like to thank the following individuals and organisations for permission to reproduce photographs:

Unit 1: p11 Kees Metselaar/Alamy; p23 Steven Day/Associated Press/PA Photos; **Unit 2:** p30 Shutterstock/Ewa Walicka; p36 Shutterstock; p45 Bob Gibbons/Alamy; **Unit 3:** p55 David Gray/Reuters/Corbis UK Ltd; p59 (top right) Martyn F. Chillmaid; p59 (bottom) Alex Segre/Alamy; **Unit 4:** p77 C.WisHisSoc/Everett/Rex Features; p85 Everett Collection/Rex Features; p97 Angela Coppola/Solus-Veer/Corbis UK Ltd; p101 Steve Wilkings/Corbis UK Ltd; **Unit 5:** p109 fotoshoot/Alamy; p113 Horizon International Images Limited/Alamy; p121 blickwinkel/Alamy; **Reading skills practice:** p132 Photodisc.

Every effort has been made to contact copyright holders of material reproduced in this book. Any omissions will be rectified in subsequent printings if notice is given to the publishers.

'Fun in the Sun' © RSPCA. Reproduced Courtesy of the RSPCA; Extract from *The Woman in Black* by Susan Hill, published by Vintage. Copyright © Susan Hill 1992. Reproduced by permission of Sheil Land Associates Ltd; Extract from *Chicken* by Mary Hoffman. Copyright © Mary Hoffman. Reproduced by permission of the author c/o Rogers, Coleridge & White Ltd., 20 Powis Mews, London W11 1JN; *The Fifth Child* Copyright © 1988 by Doris Lessing. Reprinted by kind permission of Jonathan Clowes Ltd., London, on behalf of Doris Lessing; Article 'New York Plane Crash' by Andy Rudd. Used by permission of the *Mirror*; Article 'Bargainhunter: Sauce of Discontent' by Carol Midgely from *The Times*. Used by permission of *The Times*/NI Syndication; Extract from 'Lamb To the Slaughter' from *Someone Like You* by Roald Dahl. Used by permission of David Higham Associates; 'A Case of Murder' by Vernon Scannell. Used by permission of the Estate of Vernon Scannell; Excerpt of *Mom You're Fired!* by Nancy K. Robinson, (USA, 1981) reprinted with permission by Kenneth Robinson representing the Estate of Nancy K. Robinson; Extract from *About a Boy* by Nick Hornby, Copyright © 1998 by Nick Hornby. Used by permission of Penguin Books Ltd. UK and Riverhead Books, an imprint of Penguin Group (USA) inc; Extract from *The Last Vampire* by Willis Hall. Reproduced by permission of The Agency (London) Ltd. 1981 © Willis Hall. First published by Random House. All rights reserved and enquiries to The Agency (London) Ltd. 24 Pottery Lane, London W11 4LZ info@theagency.co.uk; Extract from *Notes from a Small Island* by Bill Bryson, published by Doubleday. Reprinted by permission of The Random House Group Ltd UK; 'Poem' by Simon Armitage from the book *The Kid,* published by Faber and Faber. Used by permission; 'The Catch' by Simon Armitage from the book *The Kid,* published by Faber and Faber. Used by permission; Article called 'Oi, shoppers - that's my petrol' by Jeremy Clarkson, from *The Sunday Times*. Used by permission of *The Times*/NI Syndication; Article '12-year-old girl quizzed by three cops for an hour for trying on nail polish in Boots' by Will Payne. Used by permission of the *Mirror*; Short story 'Nemesis' by John Johns from the book *Shorties* ed. Roy Blatchford; Extract from *The Woman in Black* by Susan Hill, published by Vintage. Copyright © Susan Hill 1992. Reproduced by permission of Sheil Land Associates Ltd; Leaflet 'Kill Your Looks' used by kind permission of GASP; Extract from *Wolf Brother* by Michelle Paver, used by permission of Orion Children's Books; Excerpt from *The Lost Continent* by Bill Bryson. © Bill Bryson 1989. Reprinted by permission of Random House UK and Random House Canada; *Nineteen Eighty Four* by George Orwell (Copyright © George Orwell, 1949) Reprinted by permission of Bill Hamilton as the Literary Executor of the Estate of the Late Sonia Orwell and Secker & Warburg Ltd. Brownell; *Educating Rita* by Willy Russell, reprinted with permission of Methuen Drama, an imprint of A&C Black Publishers Ltd; 'Info for Teenagers' used by kind permission of Cafcass National Office; 'Info for Families' used by kind permission of Cafcass National Office; Extract from 'The Demon Assassin' by Alan Gibbons, from *Hell's Underground Book 2* used by permission of Orion Books; Article 'Don't let girls grow up too quickly' by Vanessa Feltz from the *Daily Express*. Used by permission of Express Newspapers; Small section of text from article 'Tea leaf stops crazed thief' from *The Sun*. Used by permission of *The Sun*/NI Syndication; Small section of text from article 'British Economy on the Brink' from *The Sun*. Used by permission of *The Sun*/NI Syndication; *Star-Crossed* Text Copyright Rachael Wing, 2007 Reproduced with permission of Scholastic Ltd All Rights Reserved; Article 'Computer Games to get Health Warnings' by Alexandra Frean, from *The Times Online*. Used by permission of *The Times*/NI Syndication; Extract from *Seize the Moment* by Helen Sharman and Christopher Priest used by permission of Victor Gollancz, an imprint of The Orion Publishing Group, London; Extract from *King* by Jon Blake; *Steel Trap* by Ridley Pearson, used by permission of the Quercus Publishing and the author; Extract from *Buddy* by Nigel Hinton. Used by permission of Orion Children's Books, London; Article called 'That awkward age…' by Kate Figes, from *The Times Online*. Used by permission of *The Times*/NI Syndication; Article 'Volunteering – The New Service' from the Duke of Edinburgh's Award Magazine. Used by kind permission of the Duke of Edinburgh's Awards; Article 'Do cell phones cause cancer?' from *The Week*, used by permission of the publisher of *The Week*; Article 'J-Bay, J-Bay' by Andrew Honey in *Zigzag Surfing Magazine* vol 7 no 4, 1983; Article called 'Harry Potter "Is too boring and grown-up for young readers"' by Charles Sweeney, from *The Times*. Used by permission of *The Times*/NI Syndication; Article 'Umbilical cords just got longer: Going to university is no longer the rite of passage it once was' by Kate Hilpern. Copyright Guardian News & Media Ltd 2008; 'Flight' by Sindiwe Magona from collection *Living, Loving and Lying Awake at Night* by Sindiwe Magona. Used by kind permission of the author; 'I Know Why the Cage Bird Sings' from *The Collected Poems* by Maya Angelou. Published by Little Brown. Used with permission; Extract from the play, *Flowers for Algernon* by Bert Coules. Used with kind permission of MBA Literary Agents.

Contents

CONTENTS

AF6 PURPOSE AND VIEWPOINT

Reading skills practice

INTRODUCTION

Breakthrough Reading Levels 3 - 6 has been written to help you develop your reading skills in a flexible yet structured way which can be adapted to you and your learning.

This book contains two different sections: Skills and Practice. You can use the Skills section to develop your reading technique and then turn to the Practice pages to assess how far you have improved. Or you can use the Practice pages to test your skills, identifying the areas you need to work on, then use the Skills section to work on them.

The Skills section is divided into the five Assessment Focuses which are not only the areas in which you will be assessed, but are also the key skills you need in order to achieve success in reading. Each Assessment Focus has been broken down into its component skills. In each of these, the book provides a series of structured activities to help you develop from Level 3 or 4, through Level 5, towards Level 6. At the end of each sequence of activities, there's a handy reminder of how the skills in each section progress from Level 3 to Level 6 so you can see how far you have come and what you need to do next.

Breakthrough has been written to improve your reading, so that you can see what you can already do, what you can improve on, and how to improve it. We hope you find it useful.

AF2 SELECT AND RETRIEVE

2.1 Fact and opinion

What am I learning?

You are learning to distinguish fact from opinion and to explore their effect on the reader.

The ability to pick out useful information from a text is an essential skill. Working out the *kind* of information you are being given is even more useful. Is it a hard, provable **fact**? Or is it the writer's **opinion**?

Identify facts and opinions.

ACTIVITY 1

fact: something which can be shown to be true

opinion: a belief which cannot be proved

1 Look at this advertisement for the Jupiter MP3 Player.

JUPITER XS

New design.
New features.
Now in 8GB and 16GB.

Jupiter X9 rocks like never before.

The advertisement makes four key points about the product.

a Which of these four points are facts which can be proved?

b Which of these four points is the writer's opinion?

Explain the effect of fact and opinion.

ACTIVITY 2

1 The advertisement on page 6 is intended to persuade you to buy a Jupiter MP3 Player.

a What effect does the writer hope the choice of facts used in the advertisement will have on the reader?

b What effect does the writer hope the choice of opinion used in the advertisement will have on the reader?

c Which do you think is likely to have more impact on readers of this advertisement – the facts or the opinion used? Write a sentence or two explaining your answer.

Explore how writers can use fact and opinion.

ACTIVITY 3

1 Look at this extract from a recent report on childhood obesity and healthy eating.

Recent research suggests that obesity in children is perhaps the most disturbing long-term health issue facing us today. It has been described as a ticking timebomb, the consequences of which will be devastating to Britain's health service over the next fifty years. Scientists have suggested that two thirds of all children will be overweight or obese by 2050 and that children today may be the first generation ever to live shorter lives than their parents.
One major concern is that foods which are high in fats, sugars and salt, known as **HFSS foods**, are continuing to make up a significant and damaging part of our diets. Manufacturers of these foods are not allowed to advertise during children's television programmes, yet they are still advertising widely during family programmes. Children obviously form a major part of the viewing audience for programmes such as the X Factor and Dancing on Ice. As a result, they are constantly being exposed to adverts for food which is actively affecting their well-being.

HFSS foods: foods which are high in fats, sugars and salt

a Look again at this statement from the first paragraph of the extract:

> two thirds of all children will be overweight or obese by 2050

Is this a fact or an opinion? Write a sentence or two explaining how you decided.

b What effect do you think the writer intended this statement to have on the reader?

c Look again at this statement taken from the first paragraph of the extract:

> obesity in children is perhaps the most disturbing long-term health issue facing us today

Is this a fact or an opinion? Write a sentence or two explaining how you decided.

d What effect do you think the writer intended this statement to have on the reader?

e Look again at this statement taken from the second paragraph of the extract:

> Children obviously form a major part of the viewing audience for programmes such as the X Factor and Dancing on Ice. As a result, they are constantly being exposed to adverts for food which is actively affecting their well-being.

Is this a fact or an opinion? Write a sentence or two explaining how you decided.

f The writer has used two adverbs in this statement: *obviously* and *constantly*. Write a sentence or two explaining why you think the writer may have chosen to use them.

g Choose one other statement from the extract. Decide whether it is a fact or an opinion and explain how you decided. Then write two or three sentences exploring the writer's choice of language in the statement and the effect this may have on the reader.

h How do writers use fact and opinion? Write two or three sentences explaining some of the different ways in which they can be used in a text.

IMPROVING YOUR LEVEL

Level 3	Level 4	Level 5	Level 6
Identify some facts and some opinions	Identify fact and opinion and make some comment on the writer's choices	Explain the effect of the writer's use of fact and opinion	Explore the writer's use of fact and opinion in the text as a whole

REMEMBER

- **Identify** the facts and opinions in a text.
- **Explain** the effect of the facts and the opinions.
- **Explore** how the writer has used facts and opinions.

2.2 Quote hunt

What am I learning?

You are learning to select appropriate quotations.

When you write about a text, you always need to give evidence to prove the point you want to make. In fact, choosing a good quotation can help you think of a good point to make – and it can help you to comment on the writer's decisions and choices.

Identify the best quotation for your point.

ACTIVITY 1

1 Look at the extract from the RSPCA leaflet 'Fun in the Sun – or is it?' on the opposite page.

   a Who does the RSPCA want to read this leaflet?
   b Why do you think the RSPCA has published this leaflet?

2 Imagine you have been asked to answer this question:

> How has the writer of 'Fun in the Sun – or is it?' tried to persuade readers to help stop animal cruelty?

Which of these quotations do you think would be most useful in answering this question? Choose **three**.

A They spend all day in the hot sun being photographed with tourists, often without food and water.

B Animals used in entertainment, particularly around tourist resorts

C Avoid going to see a bullfight at all costs.

D …people throwing goats from churches and riding horses through fire.

E This is big business in Spain, France, Portugal, Mexico and South America

Fun in the Sun

or is it?

When you travel overseas, whether on holiday or for business, you expect a wonderful experience to remember.

However, many tourists find themselves saddened and disappointed by the sights they come across.

Wherever you travel, you are likely to come across animals and many of them will not be properly cared for; some may even be abused or tortured.

Cruel entertainment

What you might see...
- Animals used in entertainment, particularly around tourist resorts, and often suffering cruelty in the process.
- Animals such as chimps and monkeys, which are often taken illegally from the wild – an act which invariably involves killing their mothers – to be used by photographers.
- During fiestas in Spain, people throwing goats from churches and riding horses through fire.

What you can do...
- Refuse to have your picture taken with any sort of animal. Chimps, monkeys, lion and tiger cubs and even snakes may look cute, but they will have been sedated with drugs to make them easier to handle. They spend all day in the hot sun being photographed with tourists, often without food and water.
- Don't take part in pony, donkey, camel or horse and carriage rides if you suspect any form of cruelty.
- Keep away from places with performing animals such as dolphinaria and circuses as places like this rely on tourists to stay in business. Often the animals concerned suffer greatly for the 'entertainment' of visitors.
- Avoid going to see a bullfight at all costs. This is big business in Spain, France, Portugal, Mexico and South America, and the money from tourists helps this cruelty to continue.

Explain your choice of quotations

ACTIVITY 2

1 Thinking about why you choose a particular quotation can help you think of a point to make about a text. For each of the quotations you chose in question 2 on page 10, write a sentence or two stating **why** you chose it.

2 Look at these points which you could use in your response to the task in question 1.

A   The writer gives lots of examples of animal cruelty.

B   The writer tells the reader what they should do to help stop this cruelty.

C   The writer makes us feel sorry for the animals.

D   The writer explains why treating animals in this way can be cruel.

E   The writer contrasts the fun humans can have on holiday with the cruelty which some animals suffer.

a Would any of the quotations on page 10 be good evidence to support and prove these points?

b Look at the points for which you do not yet have any evidence. Select quotations from the text which you could use as evidence to prove these points.

c Which do you think is most helpful **for you**: choosing your quotations first and then thinking of points which they prove? Or thinking of good points to make and then choosing quotations which prove them?

Explore the writer's choices and decisions.

ACTIVITY 3

1 When you select a quotation, try to think about any of the writer's choices on which you could comment.

a Look at this extract from one student's planning for the task:

How has the writer of 'Fun in the Sun – or is it?' tried to persuade readers to help stop animal cruelty?

By using this command, the writer is directly telling the reader what they should, or even must, do.

'Avoid going to see a bullfight at all costs.'

This emphasises the importance of the command.

b Which of the writer's choices could you comment on in this quotation?

> They spend all day in the hot sun being photographed with tourists, often without food and water.

c What comment could you make on the writer's choices which you have identified?

d Select another quotation from the text. Identify **at least one** choice the writer has made and write a comment on it.

IMPROVING YOUR LEVEL

Level 3	Level 4	Level 5	Level 6
Identify a quotation to support at least one point	Identify quotations to support a range of points	Be able to explain your choice of quotations in supporting a range of points	Explore the writer's choices and decisions in your selection of quotations

REMEMBER

- **Identify** a quotation which illustrates the point you want to make.
- **Explain** why you chose that quotation.
- **Explore** the writer's choices and decisions on which you can comment.

2.3 Skimming and scanning

What am I learning?

You are learning to select and retrieve information by skimming and scanning a text.

You do not have to read an entire text to find out what it is about. You can have a quick look over it to get a rough idea of its content, or skip through it looking for the particular information which you need.

Identify the gist of a text by skim reading.

ACTIVITY 1

1   Skim reading is when you look very quickly at a text to get a rough idea of what it is about. If you are a confident reader, you can skim read by running your eye over a text and picking out some key words. If you are not such a confident reader, one way of skim reading is to look at the first line or sentence of each paragraph.

On page 15 you will find an extract from a text. Below is the first sentence of each paragraph from it. Read them.

Chicken

The Inliners were beginning to split into two.

And now our parents were getting really concerned.

Then Alfie twisted his ankle quite badly trying to abseil down the school wall.

Then Dylan got horribly drunk doing the dare about having one glass of everything in his parents' drinks cabinet.

I tried to get Alfie to stop then, because it was clearly becoming dangerous, but he said it was Dylan's turn to dare him to do something next and he couldn't stop it because Dylan would call him chicken.

And yet we were all still in the gang.

    a What kind of text is this? How can you tell?
    b What is the text about? How can you tell?
    c What kind of people is this story about? How can you tell?
    d What do you learn about the narrator? How can you tell?
    e How do you think this text will end? How can you tell?

2 Now look at the complete extract:

The Inliners were beginning to split into two. I could feel it happening and I didn't like it. I always backed Alfie, of course, and Jamal tended to support Dylan. Leon was the most easy-going of all of us, and refused to take sides.

And now our parents were getting really concerned. Leon's had been horrified about the cat incident but he had managed to persuade them that it was just a practical joke gone wrong. The school had begun to suspect us because all the incidents were connected with our form and, being big and bad-looking, as I say, the suspicion naturally fell on us, even though we'd never done anything like this before.

The Alfie twisted his ankle quite badly trying to abseil down the school wall. I have to admit that I was helping him, but I wasn't the one who had dared him to do it. All the dares now seemed to be between him and Dylan and they were getting worse. Alfie's parents asked a lot of awkward questions about what we'd been up to after dark that made him hurt his ankle, but at least no one saw us.

Then Dylan got horribly drunk doing the dare about having one glass of everything in his parents' drinks cabinet. His sick note said he had a tummy upset, but that was putting it mildly. I overheard my mum telling Alfie's it was alcohol poisoning and Dylan had had to go to hospital.

I tried to get Alfie to stop then, because it was clearly becoming dangerous, but he said it was Dylan's turn to dare him to do something next and he couldn't stop it because Dylan would call him chicken. Dylan came back to school looking very white and shaky and I saw him give Alfie an evil look at break-time. It was hard to believe that they had ever been friends.

And yet we were still all in the gang. Inliners for ever! We were all skating along the High Street together when Dylan said to Alfie, 'I dare you to take on the Terminator.'

3 Look again at your answers to questions 1a–e. Is there anything you can add to your answers now that you have read the entire extract – or did you get the gist of the text by skim reading?

Identify key information from a text by scanning.

ACTIVITY 2

1 *Scanning* is a different reading strategy. You can use it to help you answer questions on a text. Firstly, select a key word or phrase from the question which you might expect to find in the text. For example:

> How does the narrator feel about the Inliners splitting into two at the start of the story?

Then look for it in the text.

> The Inliners were beginning to split into two. I could feel it happening and I didn't like it.

Use the technique of scanning to answer these questions. Remember to identify a key word in the question before you scan the text for the answer.

a Why does the school start to suspect the gang are behind all these incidents?
b How do Alfie's parents react to him twisting his ankle?
c What did Dylan's sick note say?

Explore a text by scanning.

ACTIVITY 3

You can also use scanning to explore a text. For example, if you were asked to answer this question:

> How does the writer's choice of language tell you that the gang's activities are becoming worryingly dangerous?

... you can scan for words which are linked to the key words in the question:

> worryingly dangerous

For example:

concerned   horrified

Identify three other words or phrases in the text which tell you that the gang's activities are becoming worryingly dangerous.

IMPROVING YOUR LEVEL

Level 3	Level 4	Level 5	Level 6
Identify the overall purpose and gist of a text by skim-reading	Identify some of the writer's key points by skim-reading a text, and specific information by scanning	Use skim-reading to identify a range of key points and scanning to identify specific information	Explore patterns in the writer's selection of key points or language by skimming and scanning

REMEMBER

- **Identify** the gist of a text by skim reading.
- key information from a text by scanning.
- **Explore** a text by scanning.

2.4 Responding and analysing

What am I learning?

You are learning to develop your response to a text and analyse it.

Skimming and scanning can help you find and use information in a text. Another way of reading is to think about the way in which the writer has made you react or respond to their ideas or their story – and then **analyse** how the writer has created this response.

Identify your responses to a text.

ACTIVITY 1

> **analyse:** to look in depth at something, identifying its different parts and their effect in order to come to a conclusion

1 Read this extract from *The Fifth Child* by Doris Lessing. After an extremely difficult pregnancy and a painful labour, Harriet has given birth to her fifth child, Ben. Lying in her hospital bed and holding her newborn baby, Harriet looks down at him.

He was not a pretty baby. He did not look like a baby at all. He had a heavy-shouldered hunched look, as if he were crouching there as he lay. His forehead sloped from his eyes to his crown. His hair grew in an unusual pattern from the double crown where started a wedge or triangle that came low on the forehead, the hair lying forward in a thick yellowish stubble, while the side and back hair grew downwards. His hands were thick and heavy, with pads of muscle in the palms. He opened his eyes and looked straight up into his mother's face. They

were focused greeny-yellow eyes, like lumps of **soapstone**. She had been waiting to exchange looks with the creature who, she had been sure, had been trying to hurt her, but there was no recognition there. And her heart contracted with pity for him: poor little beast, his mother disliking him so much ... But she heard herself say nervously, though she tried to laugh, 'He's like a troll, or a goblin, or something.' And she cuddled him, to make up. But he was stiff and heavy.

> **soapstone:** a soft stone, greenish white in colour

2 Shown below are five ways in which you can respond to a text. Read through them and then try using each approach to write five sentences about the extract from *The Fifth Child*.

1 Use your eyes	Try to visualise the scene which the author is describing.	What can I see? How do the characters look? What kinds of expressions have they got on their faces?
2 Use your ears	Listen to the characters' or the narrator's voices.	What impression do I get of these people from what they say?
3 Use your feelings	Put yourself in the character's place.	How would I feel if this happened to me?
4 Ask questions	What do you want to find out about these people, these events?	Why is he doing that? Why does she feel like that?
5 Re-read and re-think	Go back over the text and have another look.	Are there any other ways of thinking about or explaining this?

19

Explain your responses to a text.

ACTIVITY 2

1 Look again at your answers to question 2 (on page 19). In order to justify and explain your responses, you need to:

- pick out a quotation from the text which prompted your response
- then try to say **how** the writer made you respond in this way.

For example, look at this response to the character of Ben, the baby in *The Fifth Child*.

> Ben is a strange and disturbing baby.

You could use this quotation as **evidence** to **prove** your response:

> He was not a pretty baby. He did not look like a baby at all.

Then **explain** why you chose this quotation:

> It is surprising the way the writer says Ben is not pretty. It is even more surprising when we are told he does not even look like a baby. It makes the reader think that there is something very wrong with him.

- **a** Choose three of your responses from question 2.
- **b** Find a quotation as evidence to support each one.
- **c** For each response and quotation, write an explanation.

Explore any patterns in your responses to a text.

ACTIVITY 3

Sometimes you will be able to detect a pattern in a text. It might be a pattern created by:

- The writer's attitude to an idea or character – is it mainly positive or negative?

> The writer presents this character very negatively throughout the text, for example …

- The writer's choice of language – is it mainly positive or negative language? Can you make any connections between the words the writer has chosen to use?

- The writer's use of character – can you see any connections between the way the writer has written about them? Are they similar or different? What is the effect of the comparison or contrast?

> All the words which the writer uses to describe the house are connected with nature and the natural world. This suggests that …

> Juliet seems much more mature than Romeo, even though she is younger. This makes Romeo seem …

1 Re-read the extract from *The Fifth Child* on page 18. Then look at the quotations below about the character of Ben.

> He did not look like a baby at all.

> His hands were thick and heavy

> greeny-yellow eyes

> a troll, or a goblin

> poor little beast

> he was stiff and heavy.

a Can you see any patterns in the writer's description of the character of Ben and your response to it?
b Can you see any patterns in the writer's description of Harriet and your response to it?
c Can you see any patterns by comparing the two characters and your responses to them?

IMPROVING YOUR LEVEL

Level 3	Level 4	Level 5	Level 6
Identify your response to a text	Identify your response to a text, supported with some evidence or comment	Explain your response to a text, consistently supported with evidence and comments on the text	Explore your response to a text by analysing patterns in the writer's use of language or presentation of character

REMEMBER

- **Identify** your responses to a text.
- **Explain** your responses to a text.
- **Explore** any patterns in your responses to a text.

2.5 Making notes

What am I learning?

You are learning to select and record relevant information from a text.

Whether you are recording your response to a text, picking out information or quotations, you will sometimes need to make notes as you read.

Identify key points for note-making.

ACTIVITY 1

1 Read the newspaper article on the opposite page.

2 You are going to write a short summary of this newspaper article in fewer than 50 words. Below are a number of key points from the article. Select the key points that you would like to include in your summary.

A   Pilot crash landed his plane in New York's Hudson River

B   Saved 155 passengers

C   Captain phoned his wife: 'There's been an accident'

D   Captain steered jet from Manhattan's buildings, missed George Washington Bridge by less than 300 metres

E   Safely crash-landed into icy river

F   Captain helped passengers get out

G   Captain walked up and down aircraft twice to ensure no one left behind

H   Some passengers standing on wings, others plucked to safety from icy waters

I   Passengers prayed

J   Captain told passengers to brace themselves

K   Series of vessels raced to the scene

Arrange your chosen key points in the best order for your summary.

3 Now write your summary of the newspaper article in fewer than 50 words.

New York plane crash: Hero pilot Chesley Sullenberger tells wife 'There's been an accident' after crash landing in Hudson River

The hero pilot who crash landed his plane in New York's Hudson River saving the lives of all 155 passengers, phoned his wife and told her: 'There's been an accident'.

Captain Chesley Sullenberger managed to steer the crippled jet from Manhattan's buildings and miss the George Washington Bridge by less than 300 metres before safely crash-landing into the icy river.

After helping passengers to get out of the sinking US Airways Airbus 320, Cpt Sullenberger then reportedly walked up and down his aircraft twice to ensure that no one was left behind.

With some passengers standing on the wings and others being plucked to safety from icy waters, all the 155 people on board the plane survived in what was described today as 'the miracle on the Hudson'.

Passengers on the US Airways aircraft prayed as Cpt Sullenberger told them to brace themselves for a heavy landing after the plane got into difficulties shortly after take-off. He managed to land the Airbus A320 plane perfectly on the river and a series of vessels raced to the scene.

From the *Mirror*, January 16th 2009

Explore the best method for note-taking.

ACTIVITY 2

There are several different ways of making notes:

Highlighting/underlining the text you are reading	waiting to exchange looks with the <mark>creature</mark> who, she had been sure, had been trying to <mark>hurt</mark> her, but there was no recognition there. And her heart contracted with pity for him: poor little <mark>beast</mark> …

Bulleting/listing	Arguments in favour: • good value for money • does not harm environment • safe for children

Spidergram

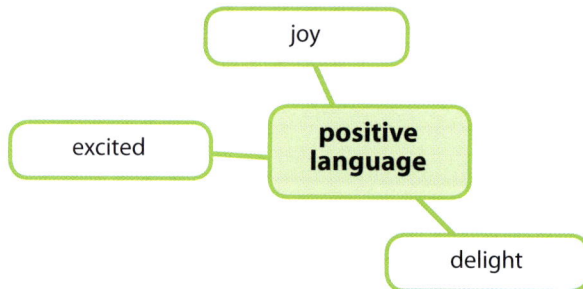

Mind mapping

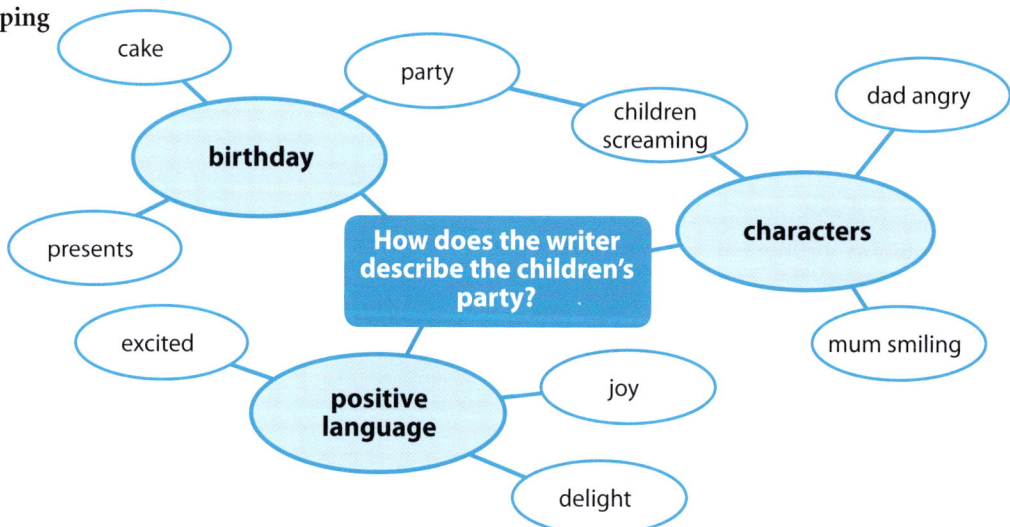

1 The question below is based on the newspaper article on page 23.

   a Which of the note-taking methods below would you use before answering the question?

> How does the writer's choice of language make the plane crash sound dramatic and terrifying?

Highlighting/underlining: I can pick out the words which I can use as evidence in my answer.

Spidergram: I can put the key words from the task in the middle and gather examples around the outside.

Bullet points/list: I can jot the answers down quickly as I read.

Mind mapping: I need to gather lots of different ideas and organise them as I go along.

   b Write a sentence or two explaining your decision.

   c Now, use your chosen method to make notes which will help you complete the task.

IMPROVING YOUR LEVEL

Level 3	Level 4	Level 5	Level 6
Identify and note some key points in the text	Identify and note most key points in the text	Identify all key points in the text, noting them appropriately	Identify all key points, selecting the most appropriate method of note-making depending on the text and the purpose of your notes

REMEMBER

- **Identify** different methods of choosing notes.
- **Explore** and choose the best method for note-taking.

AF2 Sample Answers: Levels 3–6

SELECT AND RETRIEVE

The text

This extract is from a novel called *The Woman in Black* by Susan Hill. It describes the narrator's night time journey from Eel Marsh House, an empty house isolated in the middle of the marshes, along the causeway which links it to solid land.

I had never been quite so alone, nor felt quite so small and insignificant in a vast landscape before, and I fell into a not unpleasant brooding, philosophical frame of mind, struck by the absolute indifference of water and sky to my presence.

Some minutes later, I could not tell how many, I came out of my **reverie**, to realize that I could no longer see very far in front of me and when I turned around I was startled to find that Eel Marsh House, too, was invisible, not because the darkness of evening had fallen, but because of a thick, damp sea-mist that had come rolling over the marshes and enveloped everything, myself, the house behind me, the end of the causeway path and the countryside ahead. It was a mist like a damp clinging cobwebby thing, fine and yet impenetrable... I felt confused, teased by it, as though it were made up of millions of live fingers that crept over me, hung on me and then shifted away again. Above all, it was the suddenness of it that had so unnerved and disorientated me.

For a short time, I walked slowly on, determined to stick to my path until I came out onto the safety of the country road. But it began to dawn upon me that I should as likely as not become very quickly lost once I had left the straightness of the causeway, and might wander all night in exhaustion.

reverie: dream

The question

What do you learn about the narrator's thoughts and feelings in the extract?

Identify the key words in the question.

Identify the Assessment Focus that the question is asking you about.

Reading Assessment Focus 2:

Understanding, describing, selecting or retrieving information, and using quotations

Level 3

- Sometimes I can find points which help me answer questions.
- Sometimes I use quotations which help me prove what I think.
- I use quotations to explain what the writer is saying.

> The man says he feels small and insignificant.
> He also says he feels confused when the mist comes really suddenly:
> 'I felt confused, teased by it, as though it were made up of millions of live fingers that crept over me.' He says he will stick to the path but I think he is scared and worried because he thinks he will get lost and drown.

Relevant points are selected but not developed or explained.

Some explanation but not linked to earlier points or evidence.

Effective quotation selected from the text.

Level 4

- I can find some points in the text which help me answer questions.
- I can sometimes find quotations which help me prove what I think.
- I use quotations to comment on what the writer is saying.

> The narrator is daydreaming when he realises that he is in the middle of nowhere. This makes him feel worried. He says:
> 'when I turned around I was startled to find that Eel Marsh House, too, was invisible'
> He is startled because he does not know where he is. The mist is like millions of fingers.

Point well chosen and used to answer the question.

Effective quotation selected from the text.

This evidence is not relevant in this paragraph and is not linked to a point or an explanation.

This begins to explain what the writer means but does not comment on the writer's choices.

SECTION A SKILLS LEARNING

Level 5

- I can usually find all the points which will help me answer questions. Sometimes I find these points in different parts of the text.
- I can usually find quotations which prove what I think.
- I sometimes use quotations to comment on some of the choices the writer has made.

The narrator says he is confused by the mist but I think he feels scared as well. He describes the mist:
'as though it were made up of millions of live fingers that crept over me'
This makes the mist sound really frightening, as if it was trying to frighten him on purpose.
He also feels scared because the mist came so quickly and because he is so disorientated.

> Relevant point selected.

> Well chosen evidence supporting the point which it follows.

> Points collected from different parts of the text and connected but not supported with any evidence or explanation.

> An explanation of the point and evidence but could focus more closely on the writer's choices.

Level 6

- I can find all the points which help me answer questions. I often do this by collecting information from different parts of the text, or from two or more texts.
- I always choose quotations carefully to prove exactly what I think.
- I always use quotations to comment on the choices the writer has made.

The narrator is calm at the start of the journey. He says he fell into a 'reverie'.
This suggests that he is so relaxed, he does not think about where he is or what is happening around him, which is why it is such a shock when the mist falls.
The narrator's calmness at the start contrasts with the shock of the mist which 'startles him'. He says that it 'confused, teased' which sounds almost as if he thinks it's alive. This is also suggested by comparing it with 'millions of live fingers that crept over me' which makes it sound like it is attacking him in some way.

> Well selected, relevant point.

> Effective evidence.

> Another thorough explanation focusing on the writer's choices, further supported with evidence gathered from different parts of the text.

> Effective evidence.

> Detailed explanation which is connected to the next point, comparing information from the beginning and end of the extract.

AF3 INFERENCE AND DEDUCTION

3.1 Reading between the lines

What am I learning?

You are learning to read between the lines so that you can establish the writer's point of view in their writing.

When we read, we form an idea of what the text is about by understanding what has been written. We also 'read between the lines', by thinking about the things the writer has suggested, though they may not have actually written them down.

Identify the writer's point of view: where do they stand?

ACTIVITY 1

1 Read the following extract from an article from *The Times*.

> **point of view:** in writing this refers to the way a writer sees, or views, a particular issue. Their writing will then reflect that viewpoint. It is important to remember that a viewpoint is a matter of opinion, not fact; it is not necessarily right or true!

Sauce of discontent

When I was young I may not have had the classiest of diets, counting Pot Noodle as a foreign food and tomato ketchup as more or less a vegetable … But I did know that there were some things in life so perfect in their simplicity that they should never be messed about with, such as cheese on toast, rice pudding, fish and chips and the effortless, natural bounce in Peter Purves's hair.

Fast-forward 30 years to the new age and look what's happened. They have primped and fussed with the seamless work of art that is the humble crisp and tarted it up like a collie in ringlets. Cheese 'n' onion crisps have become, inexplicably, Flavourburst Caramelised Onion and Mature Cheddar Crisps. Prawn cocktail flavour has morphed into Gourmet Tiger Prawn and Crushed Garlic. It's like putting a paper umbrella and two glacé cherries in a pint of mild, or a long leather jacket on a balding man of 50. It's embarrassing. Stop it. Crisps do not need a Thai infusion. Baked beans shouldn't come within a country mile of jalfrezi. And ketchup, well…

From the *Times*, May 3rd 2008

2 What is the writer's point of view on the way food has changed over the past 30 years? Look at the statements below and copy out the one that you feel explains her point of view:

- She thinks the new names for crisp flavours are a big improvement.
- She wishes food had been more interesting when she was younger.
- She doesn't like the way simple foods have been messed around with.
- She is glad that there are new crisp flavours available.
- She thinks old-fashioned names such as 'cheese 'n' onion' are embarrassing.

Underneath your chosen statement, write out a quotation from the article that helped you identify the writer's viewpoint.

Explain how the writer's point of view is made clear.

ACTIVITY 2

1 How would you sum up the writer's view? Copy and complete the sentence below by choosing the word you think fits best:

In this article, the writer makes it clear that she...

disapproves   dislikes   ridicules

distrusts   is disappointed with

the way aspects of the food industry have changed.

2 Look closely at the phrases and sentences from the article in the table below. What is the writer saying *more specifically* about the changes that have happened to well-known products such as crisps? Copy and complete the table below. The first row has been completed for you.

Words from the text:	Reading between the lines...	
	This makes the changes sound unnecessary	This makes the changes sound damaging
so perfect in their simplicity	✓	
they should never be messed about with		
Fast-forward 30 years to the new age and looks what's happened.		
They have primped and fussed		
the seamless work of art that is the humble crisp.		
tarted it up like a collie in ringlets		
Cheese 'n' onion crisps have become, inexplicably, Flavourburst Caramelised Onion and Mature Cheddar Crisps.		
Prawn cocktail flavour has morphed into Gourmet Tiger Prawn and Crushed Garlic.		

3 Which words made the writer's viewpoint clear? Underline the relevant words in your table like this:

Words from the text:	Reading between the lines…	
	This makes the changes sound unnecessary	This makes the changes sound damaging
so <u>perfect</u> in their <u>simplicity</u>	✓	

Explore the writer's viewpoint further: read between the lines.

ACTIVITY 3

1 **a** What is the writer suggesting about her own childhood-eating when she writes 'counting Pot Noodle as a foreign food'?
  b In the next sentence she writes 'But I did know…' What comment do you think she is making in this article about what people know these days?
  c What does the writer actually view as 'embarrassing'?

IMPROVING YOUR LEVEL

Level 3	Level 4	Level 5	Level 6
You can identify the main idea in a text.	You can identify the different key ideas in a text and you can pick out some of the details that make the ideas clear.	You can explain how details from across the text make the writer's point of view clear.	You explore how key details contribute to the overall meaning in a text.

REMEMBER

- **Identify** the writer's point of view.
- **Explain** how the writer's point of view is made clear.
- **Explore** the writer's viewpoint further: read between the lines.

3.2 What is inference?

What am I learning?

You are learning to understand the difference between **knowing** something because you have been told it by the writer and **inferring** it as a reader.

We construct our understanding of a text by taking on board **explicit** and **implicit** details: explicit details are the things the writer tells us, and implicit details are the things that are suggested. The process by which we consider suggested or implied meaning is called inferring.

Identify what the writer tells the reader: what is made explicit?

ACTIVITY 1

1 Read the following extract from Roald Dahl's short story 'Lamb to the Slaughter'.

The room was warm and clean, the curtains drawn, the two table lamps alight – hers and the one by the empty chair opposite. On the sideboard behind her, two tall glasses, soda water, whisky. Fresh ice cubes in the Thermos bucket.

Mary Maloney was waiting for her husband to come home from work.

Now and again she would glance up at the clock, but without anxiety, merely to please herself with the thought that each minute gone by made it nearer the time when he would come. There was a slow smiling air about her, and about everything she did. The drop of the head as she bent over her sewing was curiously tranquil. Her skin – for this was her sixth month with child – had acquired a wonderful translucent quality, the mouth was soft, and the eyes, with their new placid look, seemed larger, darker than before.

When the clock said ten minutes to five, she began to listen, and a few moments later, punctually as always, she heard the tyres on the gravel outside and the car door slamming, the footsteps passing the window, the key turning in the lock. She laid aside her sewing, stood up, and went forward to kiss him as he came in.

'Hullo, darling,' she said.

2 a Which of the following details does Dahl *tell* you in the extract? There is one odd one out! Copy out the details Dahl does tell the reader:

- Mary is waiting for her husband to come home.
- She loves her husband.
- She is six months pregnant.
- Someone arrives just after ten to five.

b Look at the detail that was the odd one out. What is different about this statement? Write two to three sentences to explain your ideas.

Explain what the reader can infer.

ACTIVITY 2

1 a Look closely at the following details listed in the table below. You are learning to infer meaning from the details the writer gives. What do you *infer* about Mary, based on these details? Copy and complete the table with your ideas. The first row has been completed for you.

What Dahl tells us	What this encourages the reader to infer about Mary
The room was warm and clean	She likes things to be neat and tidy.
she bent over her sewing	
Her skin – for this was her sixth month with child – had acquired a wonderful translucent quality	
She laid aside her sewing, stood up, and went forward to kiss him as he came in.	
'Hullo, darling,' she said.	

b How did you come to these conclusions? What was it in the text that encouraged you to make these inferences? Try to explain your ideas for each of the details in the table.

Explore how the explicit and implicit ideas contribute to overall impressions.

ACTIVITY 3

1 What is your overall impression of Mary Maloney? Choose from the suggestions below or think of one of your own, and write it down.

kind

feminine

pleasant

traditional

loving

gentle

old-fashioned

harmless

2 Look at the extract again. Select **one** quotation from the extract that helped form this impression. Write it down.

3 Write a point-evidence-explain paragraph exploring how this impression of Mary Maloney is created. Use the example below to help you.

A sentence to sum up your impression of Mary Maloney.

point — In the opening of 'Lamb to the Slaughter', Roald Dahl makes Mary Maloney seem like an old-fashioned housewife.

One or two short quotations to support your point.

evidence — For example, he writes that the room was 'warm and clean' and that Mary was 'bent over her sewing'.

explain — This makes it seem like she spends her time doing things to make sure her house is homely, welcoming and well looked after, things a traditional housewife would be keen to achieve. By using the word 'warm', the room is made to seem cosy and pleasant, and the fact that she seems so happy to be 'sewing' suggests that she is very content in her role as a housewife.

An explanation summing up what you **infer** from these details.

Analysis of single words and what you infer from them.

IMPROVING YOUR LEVEL

Level 3	Level 4	Level 5	Level 6
You understand the information that the writer tells you and you can make straightforward inferences based on key points.	You can comment on the ideas suggested in different details from a text.	You can explain the ideas suggested in details from across the text.	You can trace the way different details from across the text combine to create an overall impression.

REMEMBER

- **Identify** the explicit ideas the writer has given.
- **Explain** what these ideas encourage the reader to infer.
- **Explore** how explicit and implicit ideas contribute to an overall impression.

3.3 Looking beneath the surface

What am I learning?

You are learning to explore the layers of meaning in a text.

When we read, we only learn so much from the actual words on the page. Our full understanding comes from reading between the lines. We use inference and deduction to grasp ideas that a writer hints at. These reading processes involve moving away from the surface details that *can* be seen, and exploring details beneath the surface that *cannot*.

Identify what the poem is about.

ACTIVITY 1

1 Read this poem by Vernon Scannell.

A Case of Murder
They should not have left him there alone,
Alone that is except for the cat.
He was only nine, not old enough
To be left alone in a basement flat,
Alone, that is, except for the cat.
A dog would have been a different thing,
A big gruff dog with slashing jaws,
But a cat with round eyes mad as gold,
Plump as a cushion with tucked-in paws –
Better have left him with a fair-sized rat!
But what they did was leave him with a cat.
He hated that cat; he watched it sit,
A buzzing machine of soft black stuff,
He sat and watched and he hated it,
Snug in its fur, hot blood in a muff,
And its mad gold stare and the way it sat
Crooning dark warmth: he loathed all that.
So he took Daddy's stick and he hit the cat.
Then quick as a sudden crack in glass
It hissed, black flash, to a hiding place
In the dust and dark beneath the couch,
And he followed the grin on his new-made face,

A wide-eyed, frightened snarl of a grin,
And he took the stick and he thrust it in,
Hard and quick in the furry dark.
The black fur squealed and he felt his skin
Prickle with sparks of dry delight.
Then the cat again came into sight,
Shot for the door that wasn't quite shut,
But the boy, quick too, slammed fast the door:
The cat, half-through, was cracked like a nut
And the soft black thud was dumped on the floor.
Then the boy was suddenly terrified
And he bit his knuckles and cried and cried;
But he had to do something with the dead thing there.
His eyes squeezed beads of salty prayer
But the wound of fear gaped wide and raw;
He dared not touch the thing with his hands
So he fetched a spade and shovelled it
And dumped the load of heavy fur
In the spidery cupboard under the stair
Where it's been for years, and though it died
It's grown in that cupboard and its hot low purr
Grows slowly louder year by year:
There'll not be a corner for the boy to hide
When the cupboard swells and all sides split
And the huge black cat pads out of it.

2 What happens in this poem? Write out these statements in the correct order
   along a timeline of events. You will need plenty of room! Also, make sure you
   write these out **above** the line (see the example below):
   * A boy is left home alone with a cat.
   * The boy chases the cat with the stick.
   * The boy hates the cat.
   * The boy hides the cat's body in the cupboard under the stairs.
   * The boy hits the cat.
   * The boy is scared by what he has done.
   * The boy traps the cat in the door and kills it.
   * The boy uses a spade to lift up the dead cat.
   * The boy watches the cat sit, staring and purring.
   * The cat is left in this cupboard for years.

       A boy is left at home alone with a cat.

37

Explain the ideas beneath the surface.

ACTIVITY 2

1   What are the ideas *suggested* in each part of the poem? Now that you have created a timeline of the events in the poem, you are going to write **below** the timeline what each event suggests – what is the 'beneath the surface' meaning? Look at the example to help you.

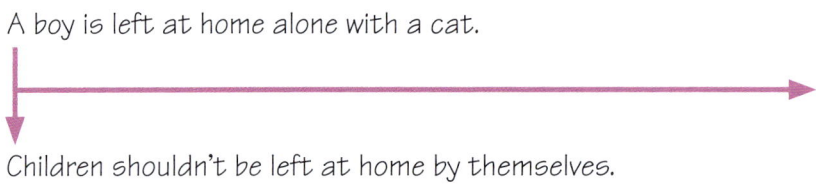

A boy is left at home alone with a cat.

Children shouldn't be left at home by themselves.

Explore the 'beneath-the-surface' ideas further: what are the layers of meaning in the poem?

ACTIVITY 3

Language is very clever! Even simple words can store a significant amount of meaning. In 'A Case of Murder', Vernon Scannell manages to use language so that the events in the poem can be read in different ways. For example, the first line of the poem could be explored as shown below.

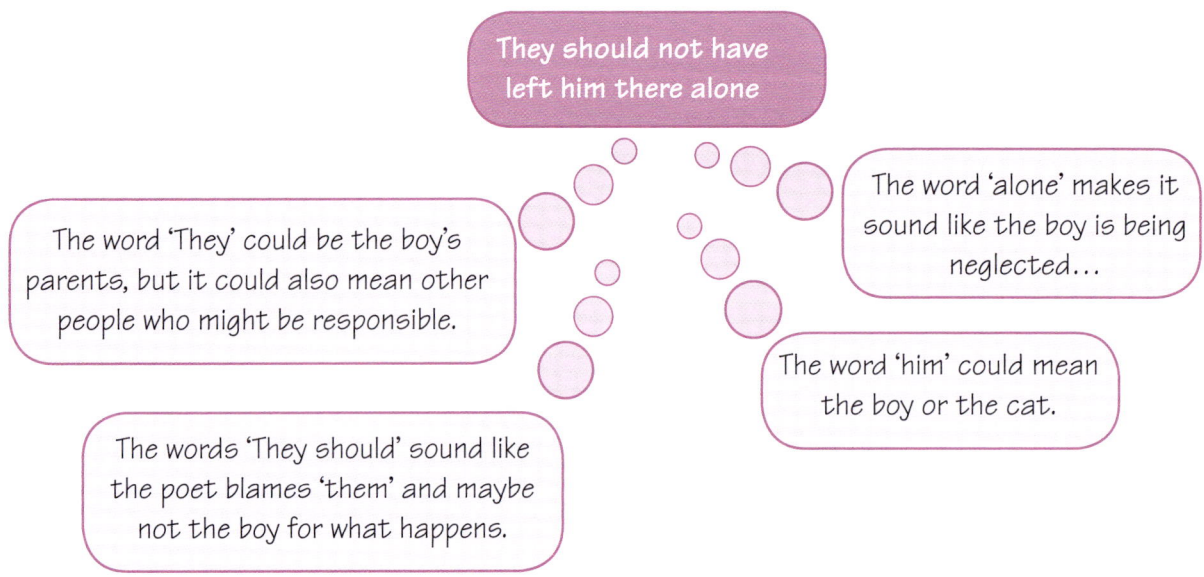

They should not have left him there alone

The word 'They' could be the boy's parents, but it could also mean other people who might be responsible.

The word 'alone' makes it sound like the boy is being neglected...

The word 'him' could mean the boy or the cat.

The words 'They should' sound like the poet blames 'them' and maybe not the boy for what happens.

1 Are there any other ideas you could add to this line from the poem? Copy out the quotation and add your own thought bubbles around it.

2 What other ideas are suggested in these lines from the poem? Copy out each quotation, and then add your own ideas in thought bubbles around it as shown above:

- He sat and watched and he hated it,
- So he took Daddy's stick and he hit the cat.
- And he followed the grin on his new-made face,
- But the wound of fear gaped wide and raw;
- There'll not be a corner for the boy to hide

3 What do you think Vernon Scannell is saying in this poem? What is his point of view? Write two or three sentences to sum up your ideas.

IMPROVING YOUR LEVEL

Level 3	Level 4	Level 5	Level 6
You understand the literal ideas in a text.	You begin to see other ideas that are suggested through the 'surface' details in a text.	You are able to explain the beneath the surface ideas in a text.	You explore the layers of meaning suggested through key details in a text.

REMEMBER

- **Identify** what the poem is about.
- **Explain** the ideas beneath the surface.
- **Explore** the 'beneath-the-surface' ideas further: what are the layers of meaning in the poem?

3.4 Themes

What am I learning?
You are learning how writers use themes to develop ideas.

The word **theme** is used in many different contexts. In films, a key piece of music is called the 'theme song'; amusement parks that are organised around one key idea are called 'theme parks'. In literature, a 'theme' is a unifying, big idea, mostly to do with experiences we all have in life, which the writer is exploring **through** their novel or poem or play. For example, the events in a novel could centre around two characters where the plot is about them becoming friends at school, but the theme being explored might be 'good versus evil'.

Identify what a theme is.

ACTIVITY 1

When you are trying to identify the theme in a piece of writing, you need to look at a range of elements:
- the plot line
- events in the narrative
- the characters.

1   Some of the key themes that recur most often in literature can be grouped under the following five headings:

rites of passage: an important life experience or ceremony that marks a change in a person, such as becoming an adult or getting married.

Significant events	Rites of passage	Difficult emotions	Relationships	Life struggles

Can you work out which heading these themes come under? Write out the headings and add each theme to the heading of your choice:

friendship   first love   betrayal   loneliness   dreams and ambitions

greed   abuse of power   death   guilt   growing up

2   Can you think of any other themes that you could add to your groups? Write them under the appropriate heading.

3 Look at the table below. If that was a plot line/event/character in a novel, what theme might that novel be exploring? Copy and complete the table selecting from the following five themes:

love   death   conflict   betrayal   greed

Plot line/event/character	Theme
A fight	
Two people falling in love	
A funeral	
A person who commits crimes for money	
Someone having an affair	

4 Now try to think of a book or film that you have seen. First, identify its main plot line, events and characters and list them as in the table above. Then, consider what theme that book or film was exploring, and write this down too.

Explain how the theme is made clear.

ACTIVITY 2

1 Read the following extracts from two different novels.

> Tina sat at the breakfast table and watched her mother making lunch for school. Her mother was putting leftover meat and salad into little plastic bowls with lids. That's what Tina and Nathaniel had to take to school every day for lunch. It was such an embarrassing lunch. If Tina sat with someone she didn't know very well, she often didn't even open her lunchbox. She wished she could have plain sandwiches like everyone else.

From *Mum You're Fired!* by Nancy K. Robinson

> Marcus knew he was weird, and he knew that part of the reason he was weird was because his mum was weird. She just didn't get this, any of it. She was always telling him that only shallow people made judgements on the basis of clothes or hair; she didn't want him to watch rubbish television, or listen to rubbish music, or play rubbish computer games (she thought they were all rubbish), which meant that if he wanted to do anything that any of the other kids spent their time doing he had to argue with her for hours.

From *About a Boy* by Nick Hornby

2   What theme do you think both of these texts share? Write one or two sentences to explain your ideas.

3   How could you tell what the common theme was? Create two columns with the following headings:

Mum You're Fired!	About a Boy

Now read back through each extract carefully and select the quotations from each that made the theme clear to you.

Explore how the theme impacts on the reader.

ACTIVITY 3

1   a   What do you feel about the situation being described in both extracts? Write two to three sentences about each extract to explain your ideas.

    b   'Identifying the theme in a piece of writing makes it easier to understand the writer's message in the piece of writing.' Do you think this is true? Write two to three sentences to explain your ideas.

IMPROVING YOUR LEVEL

Level 3	Level 4	Level 5	Level 6
You are aware of big ideas in a text.	You can see how key aspects of writing, such as characters or plot, help make the theme clear.	You can identify and explain the details in a text that make the theme clear.	You are aware of the wider implications of themes on a text's overall meaning or impact.

REMEMBER

- **Identify** what the theme is.
- **Explain** how the theme is made clear.
- **Explore** how the theme impacts on the reader.

3.5 Your point of view

What am I learning?

You are learning to develop and express a critical point of view.

Reading, and establishing the meaning of a text, is not an exact science. We can't always be completely sure of a writer's intention, and we bring our own understanding of words or experiences of ideas to texts, resulting in us making sense of what we read in very individual ways. For that reason, it is very important to be tentative when analysing and explaining the ideas in texts – we should always be open to more than one way of interpreting what we have read.

Identify the key ingredients of a point-evidence-explain paragraph.

ACTIVITY 1

1 Read this extract from *The Last Vampire* and the sample point-evidence-explain (PEE) paragraph about it on the following page.

> Without noticing, while lost in his thoughts, he had arrived outside the castle which, as the sun dipped down behind the rim of the mountain, was bathed in shadow.
>
> Henry shivered. A chill breeze had whipped up from somewhere and, inside the castle walls, an unfastened door or window-shutter was banging to and fro. There was no other sound from within and he had a feeling that the place was empty. It had a cold and lonely deserted air. Surely, if anyone had been living in the castle he would have been aware of some sort of presence by now?
>
> Continuing along the cobbled driveway, he made his way towards a pair of huge wooden gates which, he guessed, would open on to the castle's courtyard. The ancient iron-studded gates were firmly locked but a small door, let into one of the gates, groaned slightly at his touch. He pushed harder. The rusted hinges squealed complainingly, but the small door creaked open. He stuck his head through and peered around.
>
> 'Hello?' he said, nervously. 'Anyone at home?'
>
> There was no sound save for that of the breeze as it rustled, uneasily, through a pile of fallen leaves in a corner of the courtyard.

From *The Last Vampire* by Willis Hall

> **What impression has the author created of the castle?**
>
> The castle(1) is empty(2). I know this because(3) it says 'he had the feeling that the place was empty'. This tells me(4) that the place is empty(5).

2 What is wrong with the student answer above? Below are five comments about the answer. Each one matches one of the five parts of the text that are underlined. Match each number to the right letter.

   a Repeating the word used in the text shows that the student isn't interpreting the ideas in the text; they are simply repeating the words.

   b This makes it sound like there was only one reason for viewing the castle this way.

   c This opening doesn't refer to the most important word in the question: 'impression'.

   d This is the wrong expression to use for writing about 'impressions'– text doesn't 'tell' you the impression that is being created.

   e This is presenting the interpretation as fact.

3 Identify some useful rules for yourself to remember to create PEE chain answers for AF3 questions.

Explain your ideas clearly.

ACTIVITY 2

Tip!

When you are asked to consider the 'impression' a piece of writing gives you, you should think of it in terms of the picture you have in your head after reading the text. When you write about the impression, you should describe this picture in your head.

1 Look again at the question about *The Last Vampire*. What is your impression of the castle?

   a Create a table like the one below, and try to think of five different impressions you have of the castle. List them in the column with the heading 'Impression', like the example below:

Impression	Quotation
The castle seems deserted.	

   b What parts of the text helped create that impression? Look back at the extract and find the specific quotations that created the impressions you have made a note of. Write these quotations next to the appropriate 'impression' in your table.

   c What was it in the quotation that helped to create that impression? Underline the specific word or words.

2 Now choose one of your impressions from your table to focus on. Using the sentence starters from the flowchart below, write a point-evidence-explain paragraph where you explain what your impression is and how you got that impression from the text. Look at the example below to help you.

> The castle sounds like it is deserted. This is suggested with the words, 'There was no other sound from within'. By writing 'no other sound' it creates the impression that there is no living thing there other than Henry.

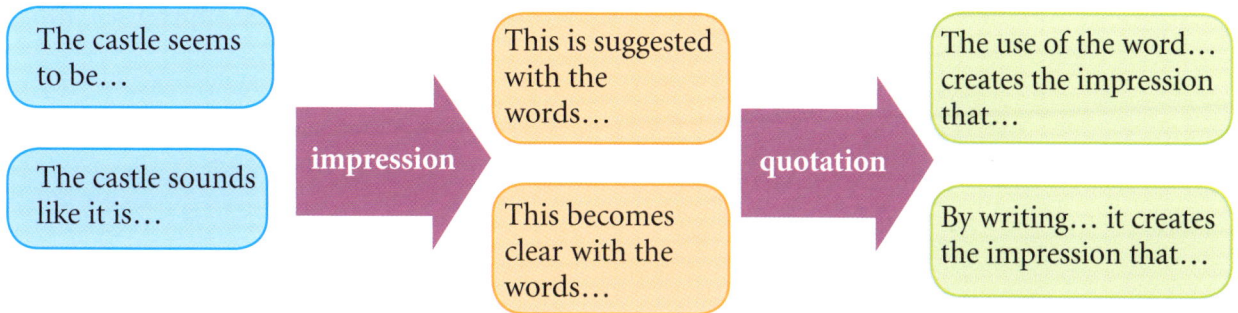

The castle seems to be…	**impression**	This is suggested with the words…	**quotation**	The use of the word… creates the impression that…
The castle sounds like it is…		This becomes clear with the words…		By writing… it creates the impression that…

Explore the text and develop your response by using modals.

ACTIVITY 3

What else could be going on in the castle? Your point-evidence-explain paragraphs will be more successful when you use **modals**. Modals help other verbs express meaning. In particular, modals show different levels of certainty. Using modals will show that you have thought about more than one possible answer.

> Key modals are:
>
> shall should will would may might
> can could must

1 Look at the example point-evidence-explain paragraph again. Which modals would work in the blank boxes? Write the paragraph out with the appropriate modals.

The castle sounds like it ☐ be deserted. This is suggested with the words, 'There was no other sound from within'. By writing 'no other sound' it creates the impression that there ☐ be no living thing there other than Henry. Also, it ☐ be that…

2 Write another point-evidence-explain paragraph of your own using one of your impressions from Activity 2. Use modals to help you develop your response in more detail.

IMPROVING YOUR LEVEL

Level 3	Level 4	Level 5	Level 6
You use the text to help you explain your understanding of it.	You make accurate Points and you use Evidence to support your comments.	You use the PEE chain effectively to explain your ideas.	You develop your use of the PEE chain effectively to help you explore the different ideas suggested in a text, e.g. by using modals.

REMEMBER

- **Identify** the key ingredients of a point-evidence-explain paragraph.
- **Explain** your ideas clearly.
- **Explore** the text and develop your response by using modals.

AF3 Sample answers
Levels 3–6

INFERENCE AND DEDUCTION

The text

Read this extract from *Notes from a Small Island* by Bill Bryson.

Daylight was fading by the time I stepped from Exeter Central Station into a light but annoying rain.

I wandered through the city examining hotels from the street, but they all seemed a bit grand for me, and eventually ended up at the central tourist office, feeling mildly lost and far from home. I wasn't quite sure what I was doing here. I looked through racks of leaflets for shire horse centres, petting zoos, falconry centres, miniature pony centres, model railways, butterfly farms, and something called – I jest not, I regret to say – Twiggy Winkie's Farm and Hedgehog Hospital, none of which seemed to address my leisure requirements. Nearly all the leaflets were depressingly illiterate, particularly with regard to punctuation – I sometimes think that if I see one more tourist leaflet that says 'Englands Best' or 'Britains Largest', I will go and torch the place – and they all seemed so pathetically modest in what they had to offer. Nearly all of them padded out their lists of featured attractions with things like 'Free Car Park', 'Gift Shop and Tearoom', and the inevitable 'Adventure Playground' (and then were witless enough to show you in the photograph that it was just a climbing frame and a couple of plastic animals on springs).

The question

Identify the key words in the question.

What impression do you get of Bill Bryson's feelings after arriving in Exeter? You should consider:
- the different things he sees and focuses on
- the comments he makes about each thing
- his tone in the writing.

Identify the Assessment Focus which the question is asking you about.

Reading Assessment Focus 3:

Deduce, infer or interpret information, events or ideas from texts, for example:
- the writer's point of view
- explicit and implicit meanings
- beneath the surface meanings
- themes.

Level 3

- I understand the straightforward ideas in a text.
- I can focus on one part of a text and make simple comments about the ideas in that part.

When Bill Bryson ended up at the central tourist office, from the words he has used you can tell he feels regretful and depressed because he says 'ended up at the central tourist office, feeling mildly lost and far from home.'

Point and explanation have become muddled together and repeat narrative content. Also, understanding remains at literal level. Evidence is appropriate.

Only one point in the text is referred to. No clear focus on question.

Level 4

- I understand ideas from different points in the text.
- I can make comments on different parts of a text, though sometimes I use the words from the text to help me explain my understanding.

Bill Bryson feels regretful when he gets to Exeter because he says 'ended up at the central tourist office feeling mildly lost and far away from home.' He has made himself regretful because he regrets leaving his home.
Another emotion he shows is embarrassment when he says 'a bit grand for me' because it's a bit too posh for him. He is feeling this way because he can't afford it.

Fairly clear point made.

Uses appropriate evidence from more than one place in the text.

Answer is relevant, but isn't fully focused on the question.

Explanation repeats narrative content or doesn't explain clearly enough how impression is made clear.

Level 5

- I make inferences based securely on what I have read.
- I can develop my explanation with ideas I have selected from across the text.

> When Bill Bryson arrives in Exeter he seems fed up. This can be seen with the words, 'wandered through the city examining hotels from the street, but they all seemed a bit grand'. He doesn't sound comfortable because he might not be able to afford these hotels.
> Then he makes it clear that he is feeling depressed and regretful. For example he says 'and eventually ended up at the central tourist office, feeling mildly lost and far from home.' This shows that he is missing home and he is regretful about coming. Also it shows that he thinks negatively about being away from home.

Uses:
- point
- evidence
- explain

to identify and explain Bill Bryson's different feelings clearly. Two points in the text referred to.

Is addressing question through response, though there is no direct reference to the question.

Level 6

- I can identify and explore the layers of meaning in a text.
- I can trace how details from across the text contribute to overall meaning.

> As soon as Bill Bryson arrives in Exeter it is clear that he feels a bit annoyed and depressed. This is made clear with the words 'I stepped from Exeter Central Station into a light but annoying rain.' Even though the rain isn't heavy, he's focusing on the negatives, suggesting that he isn't feeling very happy to start with.
> When he observes the leaflets he mentions how boring the attractions seem. For example, 'they all seemed so pathetically modest in what they had to offer'. He is also very sarcastic about some of the attractions, like 'Twiggy Winkie's Farm' because he thinks the name is ridiculous. Also, he is clearly unhappy about the fact that the leaflets are badly written. He calls them 'depressingly illiterate'. He obviously sees bad punctuation as a bad sign. Overall, he seems very unimpressed with what he sees.

Uses:
- point
- evidence
- explain

to identify and explain the different feelings Bill Bryson experiences after arriving in Exeter.

Comments on overall impression of Bill Bryson's feelings.

Last sentence shows that the question has been clearly addressed.

49

AF4 STRUCTURE

4.1 Audience, purpose and form

What am I learning?

You are learning to explore how layout and presentation are appropriate to audience and purpose.

A text should be appropriate to its audience and purpose. This is achieved through the writer's choice of language and through the choice of layout and presentation features. It's important to look at **all** of these elements before you decide what you think is the audience and purpose of a text.

Identify the audience and presentational features.

ACTIVITY 1

1 Look carefully at the leaflet opposite. Identify its:
   a audience – the people the writer is aiming the text at
   b purpose – the reason for writing the text.

> Audience is described in terms of age, gender or interests. For example:
> • teenagers
> • people who are interested in...
> • women aged 18–35.

2 How did you know? Which of the following helped you answer question 1?

   • **Content:** what the text is about.
   • **Layout:** the way the words and images are organised.
   • **Presentation:** the choice of colour, font and images.

Write two or three sentences explaining how looking at these three elements helped you – and if any of them confused or misled you.

Healthy Choices
Healthy Living

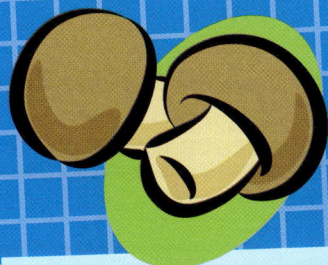

When you line up for school dinners, think about the choices you make! Healthy eating gives you all the fuel you need to make sure you keep fit and stay well.

Say YES to:

Fruit	✓
Vegetables	✓
Water	✓
Bread, potatoes and pasta	✓
Some meat and fish	✓

Did you know? Sugary drinks can make you more thirsty? The best drink to quench your thirst is water.

Did you know? You should eat five portions of fruit or veg a day to keep yourself healthy?

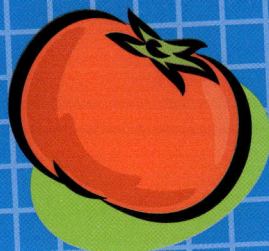

Say NO to:

Chips, crisps and other fried foods	X
Salt	X
Sweets	X
Sugary drinks	X
Snacks, biscuits and cakes	X

Explain the writer's choice of layout and presentation features.

ACTIVITY 2

1 Look more closely at the part of the leaflet shown below and answer the questions. You are learning that a writer's choice of fonts, colours, images and layout can tell you a lot about audience and purpose.

a Why is this box green?

d Why is this word in capital letters?

b Why is this writing emboldened?

c Why has this information been arranged in this way?

e Why is this symbol appropriate to purpose and audience?

Say YES to:

Fruit ✓
Vegetables ✓
Water ✓
Bread, potatoes and pasta ✓
Some meat and fish ✓

Explore the effect of the text as a whole.

ACTIVITY 3

1 How would you describe the presentation and layout of the leaflet on page 89 as a whole? Choose from the suggestions below or think of one of your own.

busy   chaotic   exciting   colourful

childish   child-friendly   bright

2 Look at the leaflet on page 51 again. Select **one** of the writer's choices of image, font, colour or layout and write a point-evidence-explain paragraph exploring how and why the writer has made this choice. Use this example to help you.

point — The audience for the leaflet is children of primary school age. The layout and presentation are colourful and child-friendly, persuading children to think about eating more healthily. — A sentence to introduce who and what the leaflet is for

— Focus on one feature the writer has chosen

evidence — In the main blue information box, the writer has chosen a font which looks like a young child's handwriting. — Because you are looking at layout, your evidence is a description, not a quotation

explain — This is designed to appeal to children because it suggests that it has been written especially for them. It also reflects the 'school theme' of the leaflet, again suggesting that it has been written for them, so making the text more persuasive.

— How does this feature appeal to its audience?

— How does this feature reflect its purpose?

IMPROVING YOUR LEVEL

Level 3	Level 4	Level 5	Level 6
Can identify the presentational features and intended audience for some texts	Can identify the presentational features and intended audience for most texts	Can make some comment on the writer's choice of presentational features and their intended effect on the reader	Can comment in some detail on the writer's choice of content, layout and presentation, and their combined effect on the reader

REMEMBER

- **Identify** the audience and purpose by looking at content, layout and presentation.
- **Explain** the writer's choice of layout and presentation features.
- **Explore** the effect of the text as a whole, linking content, layout, presentation, audience and purpose.

4.2 Poetic form

Poetry comes in a huge variety of forms. Some forms, such as *limericks*, have very strict rules on structure. Others such as *free verse* have no rules at all.

Identify the structure of the poem.

ACTIVITY 1

The elements which contribute to the structure of a poem are:

* **rhythm** – the musical rhythm formed by the pattern of syllables and words
* **rhyme** or **rhyme scheme** – the pattern in which the poet has arranged words whose endings have a similar sound
* **line length** – where the poet decides to end one line and start the next
* **verse** or **stanza structure** – lines of poetry grouped together.

1 Look at these two poems by Simon Armitage.

Poem

And if it snowed and snow covered the drive
he took a spade and tossed it to one side.
And always tucked his daughter up at night.
And slippered her the one time that she lied.

And every week he tipped up half his wage.
And what he didn't spend each week he saved.
And praised his wife for every meal she made.
And once, for laughing, punched her in the face.

And for his mum he hired a private nurse.
And every Sunday taxied her to church.
And he blubbed when she went from bad to worse.
And twice he lifted ten quid from her purse.

Here's how they rated him when they looked back:
sometimes he did this, sometimes he did that.

The Catch

Forget
the long, smouldering
afternoon. It is

this moment
when the ball scoots
off the edge

of the bat; upwards,
backwards, falling
seemingly

beyond him
yet he reaches
and picks it

out
of its loop
like

an apple
from a branch,
the first of the season.

2 What do you think these poems are about? Write a sentence or two about each one.

3 Read each poem aloud. For each poem, choose at least one of the words below to describe the:

- rhythm
- rhyme
- line length
- stanzas.

regular   measured (neither fast nor slow)

fast   irregular   slow   long   short

For example: The rhythm of 'The Catch' is irregular.

Explain the effect of the poem's structural features.

ACTIVITY 2

1 Compare the structural features you have noticed in the two poems. Why do you think Simon Armitage chose two such different structures for these poems?

2 Structural features often work together to achieve an effect, so if one feature is regular – the rhythm for example – the line length, the rhyme (if there is any) and the stanza structure may well be regular too. Look again at your answers to question 2 on page 55. Have you described any of the different structural features of *Poem* in the same way?

3 Look again at your answer to question 1 above and at the words below. Use them to write two or three sentences about how the structural features of *Poem* contribute to the mood of the poem.

The | rhythm / rhyme / line length / stanza structure | is | regular / irregular / fast / slow / long / short / measured | contributing to the | even and fluent / interrupted and stuttering / angry / joyful / sombre / excited / matter-of-fact / confused / miserable / thoughtful / chaotic / fearful / romantic | mood.

4 Repeat questions 2 and 3 looking at the other Simon Armitage poem, *The Catch*.

Explore how the poem's structural features contribute to its meaning and overall effect.

ACTIVITY 3

1 Look again at your answers to question 2 on page 55 and question 2 on page 56.

a What connections can you make between the content of *Poem* – what it is about – and the mood created by the structure?

b Why has the poet chosen to use these structural features to create **this** mood in **this** poem? Copy and complete the paragraph below to explain and explore your ideas.

Use your answer to question 2, page 55 here.

point — 'Poem' is about_____:

evidence — "_____[quotation]_____"

Choose evidence to show what the poem is about **and** the structural feature you are exploring.

explain — The writer has used [describe the structural feature] to create a _____ mood. This suggests that the writer feels that...

Why did the poet write the poem?

Use your answer to question 2, page 56 here.

IMPROVING YOUR LEVEL

Level 3	Level 4	Level 5	Level 6
Shows some awareness of poetic form	Can identify key features of poetic form, eg rhyme	Can make some comment on the writer's structural choices and their impact	Can comment in some detail on the writer's structural choices and how they contribute to the poem's meaning and overall effect

REMEMBER

- **Identify** the structure of the poem.
- **Explain** how its structural features create the poem's mood.
- **Explore** how the poem's mood contributes to the poet's meaning and point of view.

4.3 Structuring an argument

What am I learning?
You are learning how a written argument is structured.

An argument tries to convince us that we should agree with the writer's opinion. This is achieved, not just through the points that the writer makes, but the order in which the writer makes them.

Identify the argument and its structure.

ACTIVITY 1

1 Read this argument written by Jeremy Clarkson for his weekly newspaper column.

Oi, shoppers – that's my petrol

1 If I were to see someone indulging in antisocial behaviour, such as cycling on the pavement or urinating in a public place, I would roll my eyes and quietly tut. If it were something more serious, such as riding a horse through a supermarket or throwing a baby dog into a ravine, I might even say something. Strangely, however, when I spot someone dropping litter, I am overcome with a sometimes uncontrollable need to perform experiments on his head involving petrol and scorpions …

2 My suggestion is, we look hard at packaging. Three years ago there was much **brouhaha** about this – and of course the government made lots of threats and noises. Such was the outcry, in fact, that most of the big food producers and supermarket chains promised to clean up their act. I should have thought this would be a simple thing to do. A cauliflower, for instance, does not need its own Michael Jackson-style oxygen tent. It will not run off if placed on a shelf naked. Nor will it be embarrassed. Can it possibly take three years to work this out? …

3 Evidently yes, because in my local supermarket everything except the spring onions still comes in a packet of some sort … Two hundred tons of petrochemicals diverted from where they belong – in the tank of my car … In just one night at my flat in London – that's one dinner for one person – I generate enough waste to fill a hole the size of Worksop. And it makes me seethe, not because of the carbon emissions from the planes bringing it here … No. It's the fact that while I will

> **brouhaha:**
> commotion, fuss

parcel it all up and put it in the right part of the right bin on the right day for the right binmen to take to the right landfill site, thousands will simply drop it in the street.

4 And have you bought a toy recently? Every single one comes in a steel-hard plastic mould that blunts all your scissors and severs all your fingers. Seriously, you could store Britain's nuclear arsenal in the packaging used by toy companies and it would be completely safe. And then you have those plastic tie strips used to secure the product to the box. By the time you're past those the child is 28 years old.

5 So, what's to be done? Well, amazingly, you are legally allowed to remove all the packaging in the shop and leave it on the counter. But this will infuriate those stuck behind you in the queue. Or you could refuse to buy anything that has been packaged, but I fear that pretty soon you'd be naked and starving. So how's this for a plan? Companies should be fined if any of their branded litter is found on the street. This would soon encourage them to remove all unnecessary packaging. And if they found that impossible, they'd have to ensure their products were sold only to people intelligent enough to dispose of the waste properly. I'm pretty certain that if this scheme were introduced we'd have the makers of milk chocolate Bounty, Flora margarine and Kentucky Fried Chicken out of business inside a week.

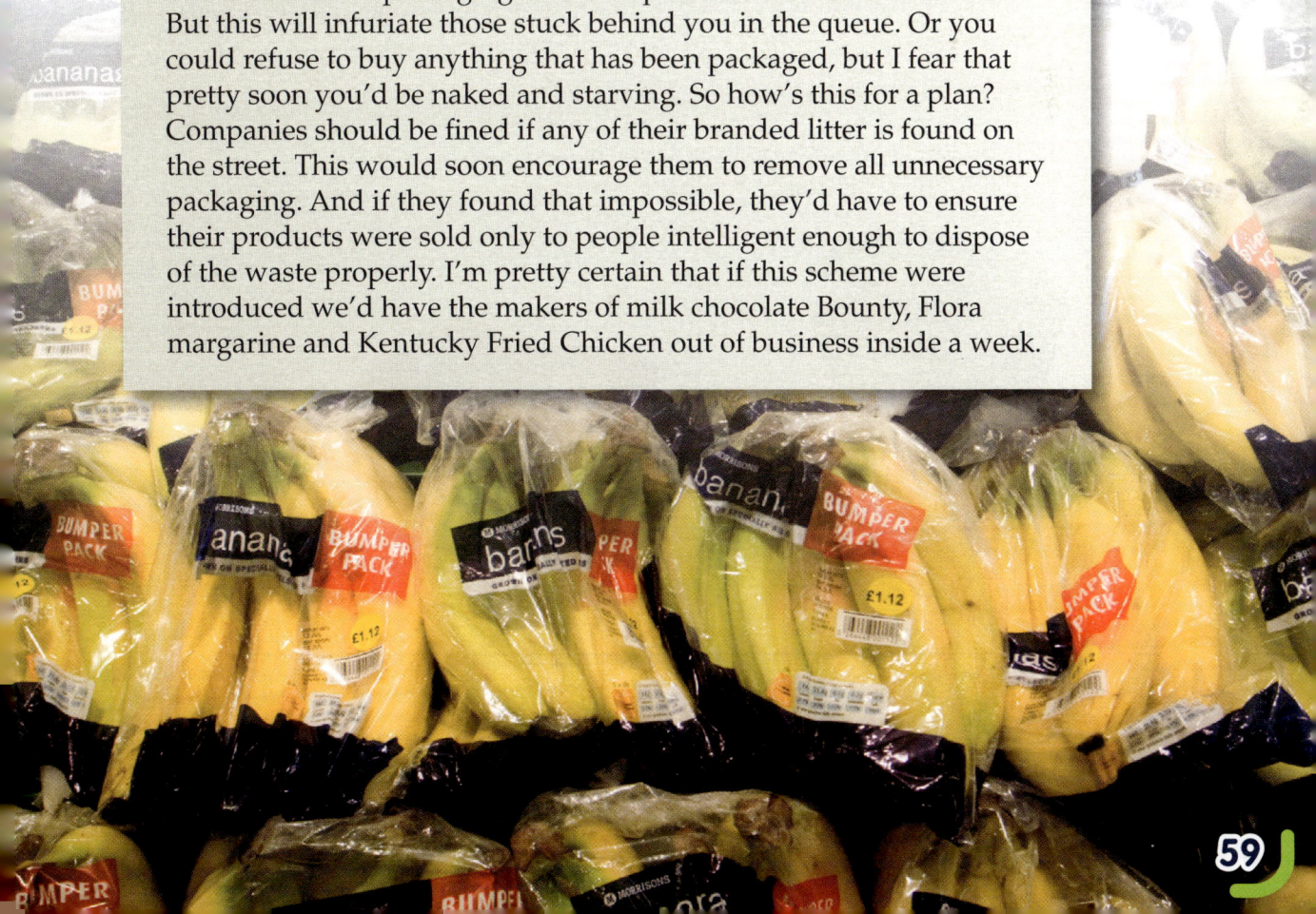

2 Sum up Jeremy Clarkson's main argument on pages 58 and 59 in one or two sentences.

3 Jeremy Clarkson's argument has three main sections:

- **The introduction** in which he explains that litter annoys him.
- **The main body** in which he makes key points to explain the causes of litter.
- **The conclusion** in which he suggests what he thinks can be done to reduce litter.

Identify which paragraphs make up these three main sections.

4 Look at A–F below. Three of them are key points made by the writer and three are the evidence he uses to support these points.

A Manufacturers and supermarkets put too much packaging on food.

D The writer's dinner creates a lot of packaging waste.

B Cauliflowers do not need to be packaged.

E Toy companies use too much packaging.

C Everything in supermarkets is packaged except spring onions.

F It takes a long time to remove a toy from its packaging.

Identify which are key points and which are evidence by sorting them into two columns.

points   **evidence**

Explain the effect of the writer's choice of structure.

ACTIVITY 2

Explains the situation which the writer feels should be improved →

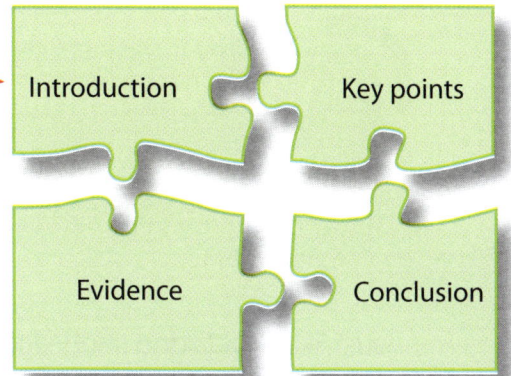

Introduction	Key points
Evidence	Conclusion

In the main body of an argument, the writer makes key points and uses evidence to support them. What does each of these different pieces contribute to the writer's argument? One has been completed to start you off.

Explore the effect of the writer's choice of structure.

ACTIVITY 3

1 The writer provides a lot of evidence to support his first main point. What effect is this quantity of evidence intended to have on the reader?

2 In his conclusion on page 59, Jeremy Clarkson makes two suggestions to improve the litter problem.

  a What are they?
  b What effect is the first suggestion intended to have on the reader?
  c What effect is the second suggestion intended to have on the reader?

IMPROVING YOUR LEVEL

Level 3	Level 4	Level 5	Level 6
Can identify some of the key points in an argument	Can identify the key points and structural features of an argument, eg introduction, conclusion	Can make some comment on the writer's structural choices and their impact	Can comment in some detail on the writer's structural choices and the effect of each element on the reader

REMEMBER

- **Identify** the writer's main argument and the different parts from which it is made.
- **Explain** the purpose of the different parts of the argument.
- **Explore** the effect on the reader of the different parts of the argument.

4.4 Narrative structure: newspapers and fiction

What am I learning?

You are learning how newspaper articles and stories can be structured.

Just like novels and short stories, newspapers tell us narrative stories about the world in which we live and things that have happened – but they use a very different structure to do it.

Identify the structure of the narrative.

ACTIVITY 1

Newspapers organise their stories using an inverted triangle structure. First, so that the article grabs the reader's attention by giving the whole story at the start; and second, in case the article needs to be shortened by cutting the least important information.

1 Read the newspaper article on the top of the next page.

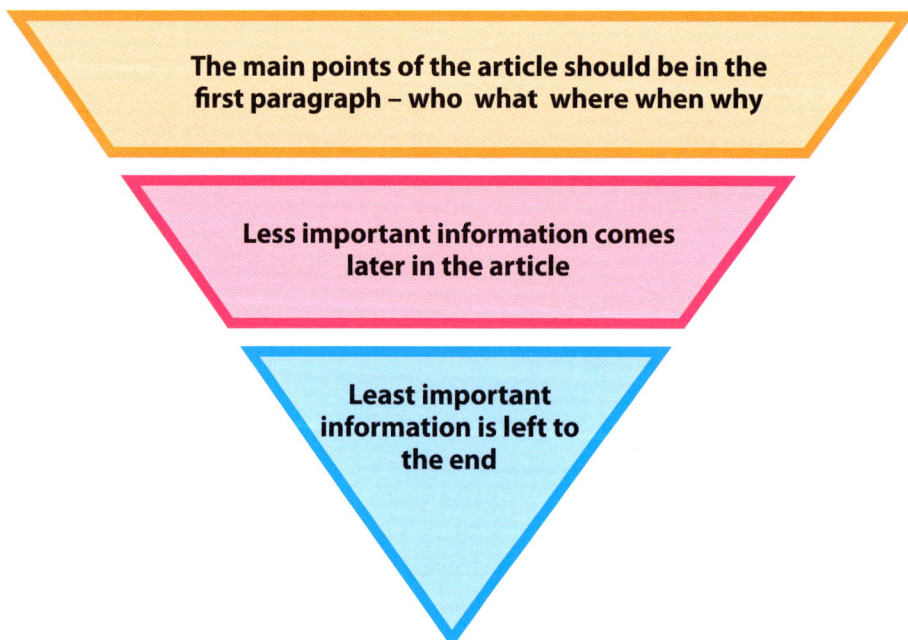

The main points of the article should be in the first paragraph – who what where when why

Less important information comes later in the article

Least important information is left to the end

12-year-old girl quizzed by three cops for an hour for trying on nail polish in Boots

A girl was quizzed by three policemen and held for over an hour after dabbing a shop's nail polish on her thumb.

Hannah Gilbert, 12, tried on the cosmetic when there were no testers available. To her amazement, a security guard warned her she must pay for it – or it was theft.

Hannah had no money and was hauled into the back office at Boots. The sobbing schoolgirl was then questioned by three PCs and only freed after her parents arrived and paid for the £6.29 Revlon peach polish.

Mum Cheryl, 46, of Folkestone, Kent, said: 'Hannah was scared and crying. The whole approach was over the top. At first there were three officers and when we got there it was one.' Hannah added: 'I was really scared.'

Boots said: 'We worked with Miss Gilbert and police to ensure an effective resolution.'

Kent police added: 'No crimes were reported and no further action taken.'

From the Mirror, *July 2008*

2 The article above is 171 words long. If you had to shorten it, how much information would be lost by cutting:

   a the last paragraph
   b the paragraph before that
   c the one before that
   d and so on?

3 Narrative fiction – a story – follows a much more linear structure. Read this very short story.

Nemesis

They watched the old man collect his pension, followed him like twin hawks, closed on him with practised skill.

Startled, the victim fell clutching his attackers who found themselves stumbling backwards off the pavement into heavy traffic.

The Coroner said 'Accidental Death.' The old man, once a Commando, knew better.

4 Fiction – novels and short stories – often uses a four-part structure.

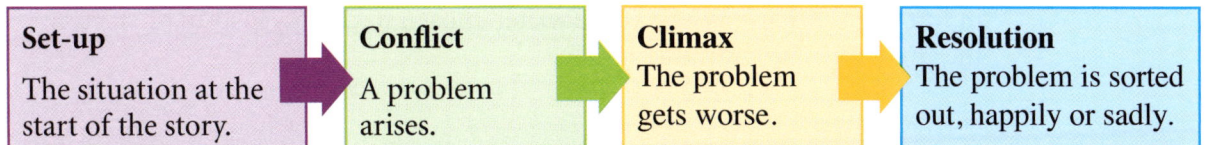

Set-up
The situation at the start of the story.

Conflict
A problem arises.

Climax
The problem gets worse.

Resolution
The problem is sorted out, happily or sadly.

For example:

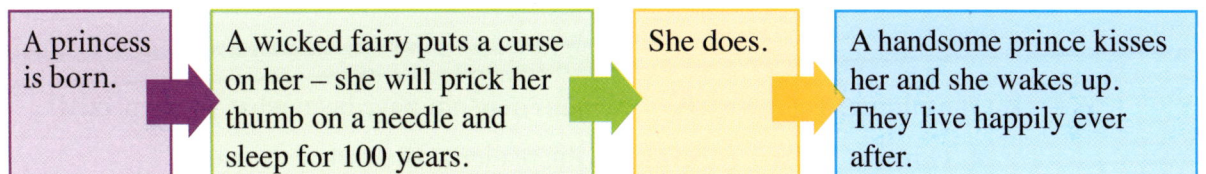

A princess is born.

A wicked fairy puts a curse on her – she will prick her thumb on a needle and sleep for 100 years.

She does.

A handsome prince kisses her and she wakes up. They live happily ever after.

Identify these four stages in the story, *Nemesis*.

A

B

C

D

Explain the effect of the narrative structure on the reader.

ACTIVITY 2

1 The writer of *Nemesis* has begun the story by giving the set-up and the conflict in just one sentence. Why has the writer chosen to do this instead of starting the story with, for example:

> An elderly man walked into the post office to collect his pension. A long queue stretched from the counter to the door. The man sighed and settled down to wait.

2 The ending, or *resolution*, of *Nemesis* may not have been what you expected.

   a **How** has the writer surprised the reader at the end of the story?
   b **Why** has the writer surprised the reader at the end of the story?

Explore the writer's choices in manipulating narrative structure.

ACTIVITY 3

1   Although fiction usually uses the four-part structure you looked at earlier, writers sometimes use flashbacks to control their readers' response to the story. What might be the effect on the reader if the writer had used this structure:

  a   climax ⟶ set-up ⟶ conflict ⟶ resolution
  b   resolution ⟶ set-up ⟶ conflict ⟶ climax

2   Which of the different structures you have looked at – including the structure that the writer used – is the most effective in creating:

  a   a surprise ending
  b   a build-up of tension
  c   an attention-grabbing opening?

IMPROVING YOUR LEVEL

Level 3	Level 4	Level 5	Level 6
Can identify some of the key stages in a narrative	Can identify the four stages in a narrative	Can make some comment on the effect of the narrative structure on the reader	Can comment in some detail on the likely effect of a range of narrative structures on the reader

REMEMBER

- **Identify** the structure of the narrative.
- **Explain** the effect of the narrative structure on the reader.
- **Explore** the structural choices the writer has made to manipulate the reader's response to the story.

4.5 Sentence structure

What am I learning?

You are learning how writers use different sentence types and lengths to create atmosphere and emphasis.

Writers use a range of sentence types and sentence structures to create different effects and to make their writing more varied and interesting.

Identify the range of sentence types a writer has chosen to use.

ACTIVITY 1

1 Read the following extract from *The Woman in Black* by Susan Hill.

Arthur Kipps is staying overnight in an isolated old house with only a dog for company. During the day, he found a locked door that had no keyhole, let alone a key to unlock it. From inside the room he heard strange noises. Now that darkness has fallen, he finds himself strangely drawn back to the locked room.

> The door of the room from which the noise came, the door which had been securely locked, so that I had not been able to break it down, the door to which there could not be a key – that door was now standing open. Wide open.
>
> Beyond it lay a room, in complete darkness, **save for** the first yard or two immediately at the entrance, where the dim light from the bulb on the landing outside fell onto some brown, shining floor covering. Within, I could hear both the noise – louder now because the door was open – and the sound of the dog, pattering anxiously about and sniffing and snuffling as she went.
>
> I do not know how long I stood there in fear and trembling and in dreadful bewilderment. I lost all sense of time and ordinary reality. Through my head went a tumbling confusion of half-thoughts and emotions, visions of spectres and of real fleshy intruders, ideas of murder and violence, and all manner of odd, distorted fears. And, all the time, the door stood wide open and the rocking continued. Rocking. Yes. I came to, because I had realised at last what the noise within the room was – or at least what it reminded me of closely. It was the sound of the wooden runners of my **nurse**'s rocking chair, when she had sat beside me every night while I went to sleep, as a small child, rocking, rocking.

save for: except for

nurse: nanny

2 Identify the overall effect on the reader that the writer is trying to create in this extract.

3 Writers can use:

- long, compound or complex sentences to give detail or to build up tension
- short, simple sentences to create emphasis or a feeling of shock or surprise
- short, incomplete sentences (which either do not have a main verb or a subject) to create an even greater emphasis or feeling of shock or surprise.

a What different kinds of sentences has the writer chosen to use in this extract?

b Write down an example of each of the sentence types that you identified.

Explain the effect the writer creates using a range of sentence types.

ACTIVITY 2

1 Look again at the first paragraph of the extract on page 66.

> The door of the room from which the noise came, the door which had been securely locked, so that I had not been able to break it down, the door to which there could not be a key – that door was now standing open. Wide open.

a How many sentences are there in this paragraph?
b Compare the lengths of these sentences. What do you notice?
c What is the effect of this *contrast* on the reader?

2   Look again at the first sentence of the extract on page 66. The writer builds up this long sentence by adding clause after clause, each one adding more information.

the first clause | The door of the room from which the noise came,

the second clause | the door which had been securely locked, so that I had not been able to break it down,

the third clause | the door to which there could not be a key –

the fourth clause | that door was now standing open.

What is the effect of this build up to the fourth and final clause? To help you, try reading the whole sentence aloud, using as much expression as possible.

Explore the effect of the writer's sentence construction.

ACTIVITY 3

The order in which a writer organises the clauses in a sentence can change the effect that they create.

1   Look again at the different clauses in the final sentence from the extract on page 66.

It was the sound of the wooden runners of my nurse's rocking chair,

when she had sat beside me every night while I went to sleep,

as a small child,

rocking,

rocking.

a   What effect does the final repetition of the word *rocking* create?

b How are the emphasis and effect of the sentence changed if you shuffle the clauses round like this:

It was the sound of the wooden runners of my nurse's rocking chair,

rocking,

rocking,

when she had sat beside me every night while I went to sleep,

as a small child.

c Try rearranging the clauses of the first sentence from the extract, which you looked at in question 2 at the top of page 68. How many different ways can it be done? How does each one change the emphasis and effect of the sentence?

IMPROVING YOUR LEVEL

Level 3	Level 4	Level 5	Level 6
Can identify some of the different sentence types in a text	Can identify most of the different sentence types in a text and comment on the effect of some	Can comment on the effect of a range of sentence types, eg long and short, simple and complex sentences	Can comment in some detail on the effect of a range of sentence types and the way in which the writer has chosen to construct them

REMEMBER

- **Identify** the sentence types which the writer has chosen to use.
- **Explain** the effect on the reader of each sentence type.
- **Explore** the writer's choice of sentence construction and its intended effect on the reader.

STRUCTURE

AF4 Sample Answers:
Levels 3–6

The text

Look at the cover of this leaflet which aims to persuade people not to smoke.

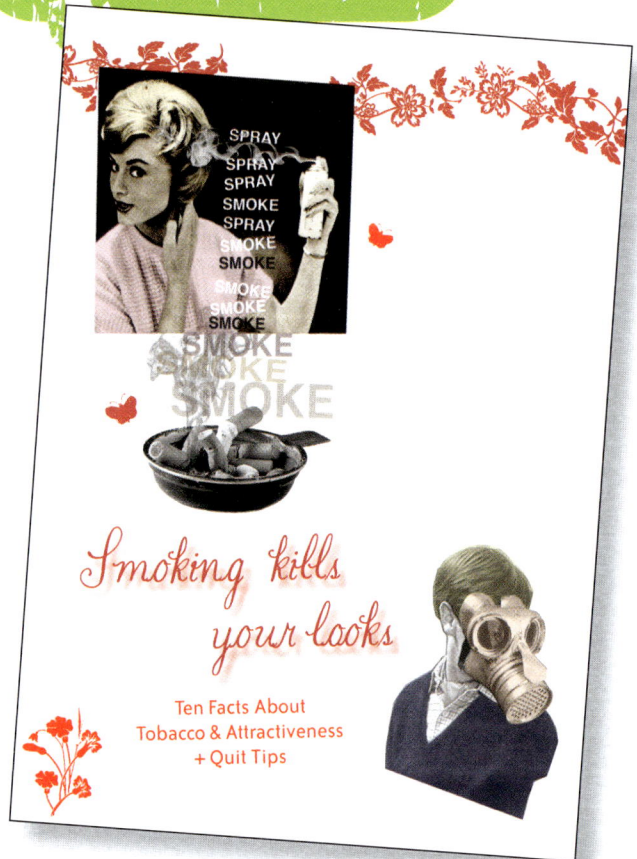

SPRAY
SPRAY
SPRAY
SMOKE
SPRAY
SMOKE
SMOKE
SMOKE
SMOKE
SMOKE
SMOKE
SMOKE

Smoking kills your looks

Ten Facts About
Tobacco & Attractiveness
+ Quit Tips

The question

Identify the key words in the question.

How does the presentation of this text encourage people not to smoke? You should comment on:
- the intended audience
- the layout
- the use of colour, images and fonts.

Identify the Assessment Focus that the question is asking you about.

Reading Assessment Focus 4:

Identifying and commenting on the structure and organisation of texts, for example:
- the points or events which a writer chooses to focus on
- the order in which events or points are structured
- how the writer builds to an ending
- the effect of the writer's choice of sentence length.

Level 3

- I can identify some of the key points or features in a text.
- Sometimes I find it difficult to explain why the writer has chosen to do this.

> The leaflet makes smoking look really disgusting by putting a picture of a dirty ashtray. The man has a gas mask on because of the bad smell of smoke. It says smoking kills your looks which means that you won't look very good if you smoke.

Identifies some relevant key features of the text...

...but it does not answer the question. The question asks you to comment on **presentation,** not on the use of **language.**

Level 4

- I can identify how the writer has structured a text.
- I can sometimes comment on why the writer has decided to do this.

> The woman is spraying smoke on her hair and the writing is in pink which appeals to women so I think the audience for the leaflet is women. The ashtray is full of cigarette butts and is in the centre of the leaflet. The word 'smoke' is in grey so it looks like smoke and it is going up, onto the picture of the woman.

Identifies some key features of the text.

Explains why the writer has made this choice and the effect it has on the reader.

The effect of these features is not fully explained.

Level 5

- I can identify the key ideas in a text and the order in which the writer has put them.
- I can usually explain why the writer has made these decisions.

> The leaflet is aimed at women, persuading them to give up smoking. At the centre of the advert is a full ashtray and the smoke is making the woman in the picture smell. The man is wearing a gasmask. The man and the woman are in opposite corners which suggests that he wants to get as far away from her as possible because she smells of smoke. This is to make women think that men will not like them if they smell of smoke.

Uses:
- point
- evidence
- explain

to identify and explain the writer's choices.

Comments on the layout of the text and its intended effect on the audience.

Level 6

- I can identify how a writer has structured and sequenced their points or ideas in a text.
- I can comment on the effect the writer wants to have on the reader and how their choice of structure and organisation helps achieve this.

> When you first look at the leaflet, there are lots of things which look romantic and designed to appeal to women. The writing is in pink and the woman is spraying her hair to look attractive and there are pink flowers and butterflies around her, all of which stereotypically appeals to women.
> But when you look closely you notice more negative things. The woman is spraying her hair with smoke, and the man in the picture is wearing a gasmask and is as far away from her as he can get. This suggests that smoking smells stronger than spray or perfume and that men will not like the smell and will not like women who smell of smoke. The layout of the leaflet first makes you look and then makes you think that smoking is horrible.

Uses:
- point
- evidence
- explain

to identify and explain several of the writer's choices.

Comments in detail on the overall effect of the leaflet on the reader and how it achieves its purpose.

AF5 LANGUAGE

5.1 The best words

What am I learning?

You are learning to identify when writers have chosen language for effect and how to comment on it.

Writers do not write by accident: they choose the words they write very carefully. They draft, re-draft and keep re-drafting until they have found the best words and put them in the best order to achieve the effect they want to create.

Identify when a writer has chosen language for effect.

ACTIVITY 1

1 Read this paragraph from the opening chapter of *Wolf Brother* by Michelle Paver.

> The fire had burned low. He crouched in the fragile shell of light and peered into the looming blackness of the Forest. He couldn't see anything. Couldn't hear anything. Had it come back? Was it out there now, watching him with its hot, murderous eyes?

Now read this:

> The fire was low. He sat in the light and looked into the dark forest. He couldn't see anything. Couldn't hear anything. Had it come back? Was it out there now, watching him?

2 Both texts describe the scene and tell you what is happening. How are the two texts different?

3 Pick out **three** words or phrases which have been left out of the second text.

4 Is one text better than the other? Why?

Explain the writer's choice of language.

ACTIVITY 2

1 Writers choose their words to make the reader think and feel in different ways. Write a sentence or two explaining your thoughts and feelings about the boy in the forest.

2 Can you identify any words or phrases in the text which made you think or feel this way?

Explore the writer's choice of language.

ACTIVITY 3

1 Sometimes writers choose words because of ideas or feelings we associate with them. These are called the *connotations* of that word.

Choose three of the words, or three words from the phrases you chose in question 3 above, think about their meaning and what else they make you think of. You can organise your ideas in the same way as this example.

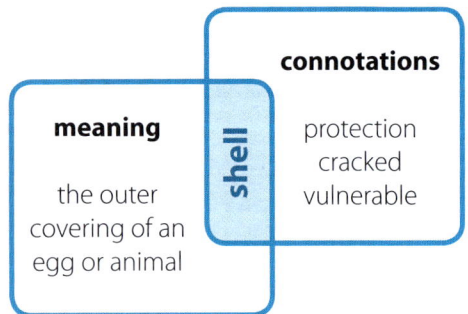

meaning	shell	**connotations**
the outer covering of an egg or animal		protection cracked vulnerable

2 When you write about a writer's choice of language, you can use a point-evidence-explain paragraph. The most difficult part to write is the 'explain' or 'comment on language'. Remember to comment on the connotations of the language used, what the writer is doing, and how it makes the reader feel or think. Look at the example on the following page.

point — Michelle Paver describes the boy at the start of the book sitting alone in the forest:

evidence — "The fire had burned low. He crouched in the fragile shell of light and peered into the looming blackness of the forest."

explain — Describing the light from the fire as a "fragile shell" — connotation
suggests that, like the shell of an animal or an egg, it protects the boy from the dangers of the forest and the darkness. Because it is "fragile", the writer is — What the writer is doing
emphasising the danger that the boy is in. The shell may not be strong enough to protect him. This gives the — effect on reader
reader a feeling of danger and tension, wondering what will happen to the boy.

3 Choose one of the words or phrases you identified in question 3 on page 74. Use a table like the one below to prepare your comment on the writer's choice of language.

Word or phrase	Connotations	What the writer is doing	The effect on the reader

IMPROVING YOUR LEVEL

Level 3	Level 4	Level 5	Level 6
Identify one or two examples of descriptive language	Identify and make some undeveloped comments on one or two examples of descriptive language	Explain the writer's choice of language and its likely effect on the reader	Explore the writer's choice of language in more detail, commenting on its connotations and its likely effect on the reader

REMEMBER

- **Identify** the words that the writer has chosen for effect.
- **Explain** how they make the reader feel or think.
- **Explore** how the writer has done this.

5.2 Selecting and connecting language

What am I learning?

You are learning how writers select vocabulary for its effect on the reader.

It can be difficult to identify the language which a writer has chosen for effect – and which you can use to make an effective comment.

Identify the writer's choice of language.

ACTIVITY 1

Bill Bryson is an American who has lived in Britain for much of his adult life. In his book *The Lost Continent* he drives across the United States, writing about his experiences.

1 Read this extract in which he explains his thoughts about the farmers of the Midwest states.

There is scarcely a farmer in the Midwest over the age of twenty who has not at some time or other had a limb or digit yanked off and thrown into the next field by some noisy farmyard implement. To tell you the absolute truth, I think farmers do it on purpose. I think working day after day beside these massive threshers and balers with their grinding gears and flapping fan belts and complex mechanisms they get a little hypnotised by all the noise and motion. They stand there staring at the whirring machinery and they think, 'I wonder what would happen if I just stuck my finger in there a little bit.'...

My grandfather was just the same. He would often be repairing the car when the jack would slip and he would call out to you to come and crank it up again as he was having difficulty breathing, or he would run over his foot with the lawn-mower, or touch a live wire ... leaving himself unscathed apart from a ringing in the ears and a certain lingering smell of burnt flesh. Like most people from the rural Midwest, he was practically indestructible. There are only three things that can kill a farmer: lightning, rolling over in a tractor, and old age. It was old age that got my grandfather.

2 One way of thinking about a writer's choice of language is to divide their words into two groups:

- words which make the writing make sense, for example, 'of', 'the', 'and'
- words which explain and describe.

Look again at this sentence from the extract on page 76:

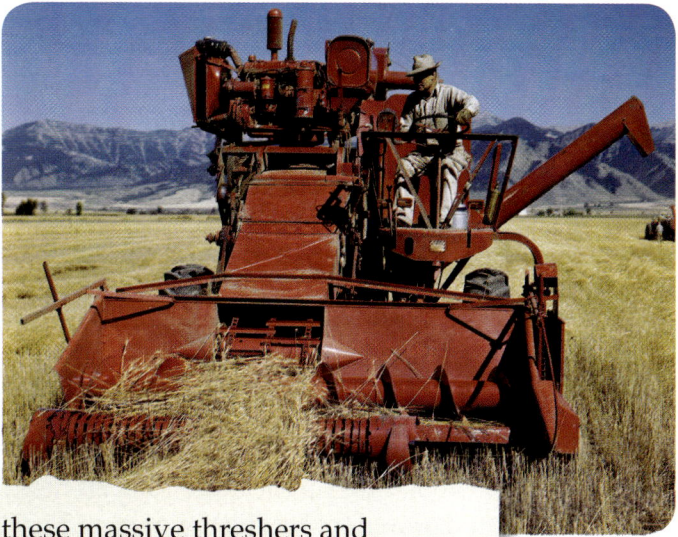

> I think working day after day beside these massive threshers and balers with their grinding gears and flapping fanbelts and complex mechanisms they get a little hypnotised by all the noise and motion.

Divide all the words from the extract into two groups. Put them in a table like the one below.

Words/phrases to help the writing make sense	Words/phrases which explain and describe
I	working
think	day after day
beside	massive
these	threshers

Explain the effect the writer wanted to achieve.

ACTIVITY 2

1 Look again at this phrase from the extract:

> balers with their grinding gears

The writer has chosen to use the word 'grinding' to describe the gears of the farming machinery. If you look up the word 'grinding' (or 'grind') in a thesaurus, you will find a list of words with a similar meaning:

grind

crush	mince
pulverise	gnash
break up	scrape

a Which of these words do you think the writer could have chosen to use instead of 'grind'?

b Which one do you think is the most effective word?

c Write a sentence or two explaining why you chose that word.

d Compare the word you chose with the word the writer chose. Write a sentence or two explaining the effect the writer wanted to achieve by choosing the word 'grinding'.

Explore why the writer chose this language.

ACTIVITY 3

1 Look again at the describing and explaining words you identified in the extract in question 2 at the top of page 77. They can be divided again, into groups. Which words would you put in each group? Some words might appear in more than one group – and some might not appear in any. Make a table like the one below and organise the words under the headings given. Some words have been added already to get you started.

Machinery	Power	Danger
threshers	massive	grinding

2 What impression do you think Bill Bryson wanted to give the reader in this extract of:

- farm machinery
- farmers?

You could use these sentence starters to help you:

> All the words that the writer has chosen to describe the farm machinery suggest that...
> This emphasises the writer's point that farmers...

3 Look again at the extract on page 76.

a What impression of his grandfather is the writer trying to give the reader?

b Choose **one** word which you feel contributes to this impression.

c Use a thesaurus or your own vocabulary to find a range of alternatives the writer could have chosen. Select the best one.

d How would the effect of the writer's choice of language be changed if you replaced the writer's choice with your choice?

e Write a sentence or two exploring the writer's choice. You could start with:
   The writer has chosen to use the word '___'. This suggests that...

f Can you connect this word to any others the writer has chosen to use?

IMPROVING YOUR LEVEL

Level 3	Level 4	Level 5	Level 6
Identify one or two examples of language which the writer has chosen	Identify and make some undeveloped comments on one or two examples of language which the writer has chosen	Explain the writer's choice of language and its likely effect on the reader	Explore the connections in the writer's choice of language, its connotations and implications for the text as a whole

REMEMBER

- **Identify** the descriptive language the writer has chosen to use.
- **Explain** the effect of at least one word the writer has chosen to use.
- **Explore** the connections in the writer's choice of language and what they suggest.

5.3 Mood

> **What am I learning?**
> You are learning how writers use language to create atmosphere.

Writers use character and setting to establish the atmosphere or mood of a piece of writing. One way to think about the mood the writer has created is to imagine the kind of voice you might use if you were reading the text aloud.

Identify the language the writer has used to create atmosphere.

ACTIVITY 1

1984 is a novel written by George Orwell in 1949. It describes a world of the future, ruled by Big Brother who is constantly watching everything that everyone does. No one is allowed to disagree with Big Brother – or even to think negatively about him. Those who do so are *thought criminals* and are taken by the *Thought Police*.

1 Read this extract from the opening of George Orwell's novel, *1984*.

BIG BROTHER IS
WATCHING YOU

> It was a bright cold day in April, and the clocks were striking thirteen. Winston Smith, his chin nuzzled into his breast in an effort to escape the vile wind, slipped quickly through the glass doors of Victory Mansions, though not quickly enough to prevent a swirl of gritty dust from entering along with him.
>
> The hallway smelt of boiled cabbage and old rag mats. At one end of it a coloured poster, too large for indoor display, had been

tacked to the wall. It depicted simply an enormous face, more than a metre wide: the face of a man of about forty-five, with a heavy black moustache and ruggedly handsome features. Winston made for the stairs. It was no use trying the lift. Even at the best of times it was seldom working, and at present the electric current was cut off during daylight hours. It was part of the economy drive in preparation for Hate Week. The flat was seven flights up, and Winston, who was thirty-nine and had a varicose ulcer above his right ankle, went slowly, resting several times on the way. On each landing, opposite the lift-shaft, the poster with the enormous face gazed from the wall. It was one of those pictures which are so contrived that the eyes follow you about when you move. BIG BROTHER IS WATCHING YOU, the caption beneath it ran.

2 Look at the words below.

depression   misery   oppression

disturbing   danger   sinister

Which **one** word best describes the mood Orwell has created in the extract on page 118? Use one of the sentences below to help you structure your answer.

In the opening of 1984, Orwell creates a depressing mood.

In the opening of 1984, Orwell creates a mood of depression.

Explain how the writer creates this atmosphere.

ACTIVITY 2

1 Orwell has selected lots of detail to describe the setting of the novel. For example:

- the clocks were striking thirteen
- vile wind
- swirl of gritty dust

Make a list of all the details which Orwell describes in the opening.

2 Which details help to create the mood you identified in question 2?

Explore how the writer creates this atmosphere.

ACTIVITY 3

1 Are any of the details you selected in question 4 similar in any way? For example, they might have the same effect on the reader or describe similar things.

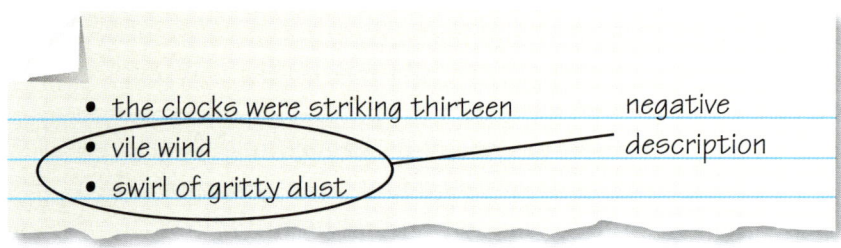

- the clocks were striking thirteen   negative
- vile wind   description
- swirl of gritty dust

2 Choose two or three of the details you selected in Activity 2. What do they suggest to you? You can write your answers in spider diagrams like the ones below

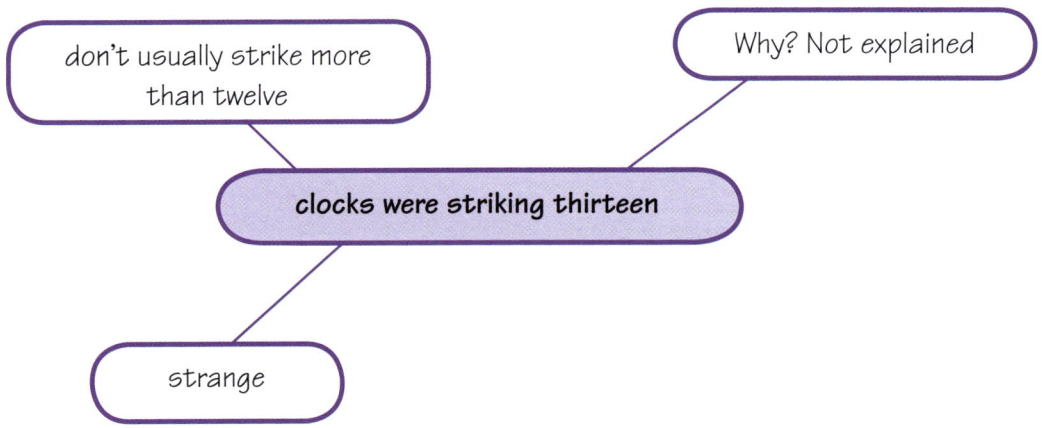

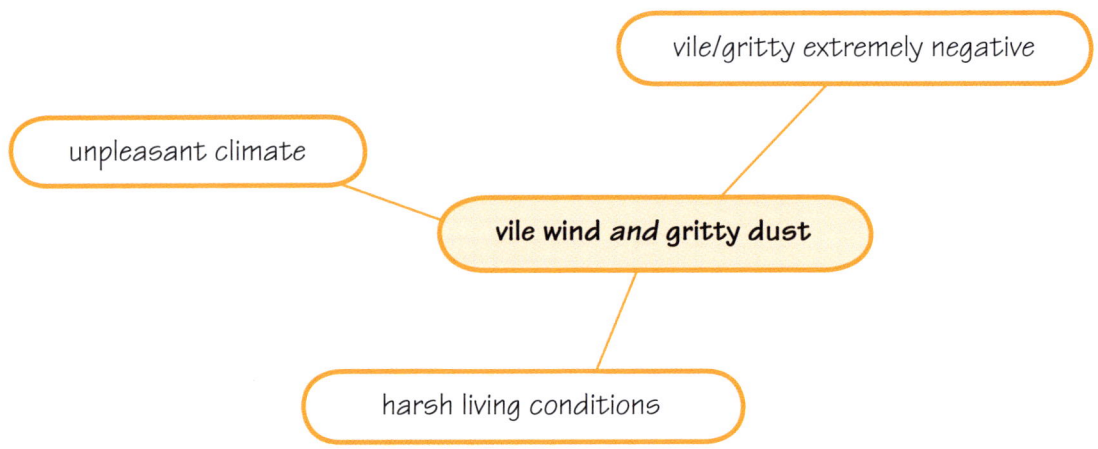

don't usually strike more than twelve

Why? Not explained

clocks were striking thirteen

strange

vile/gritty extremely negative

unpleasant climate

vile wind _and_ gritty dust

harsh living conditions

3 Read this paragraph in which a student writes about the atmosphere at the start of *1984*.

point — In the opening of 1984, Orwell creates a disturbing mood:

evidence — 'the clocks were striking thirteen'

explain — Usually we expect clocks to strike no more than twelve times. Orwell is showing the reader that this world is similar to but very different from our own, and that life has changed in the future. He does not explain why this change has happened, which makes it seem strange and a little worrying.

Why does this detail explain the point?

What the writer is doing.

effect on reader

4 Write a point-evidence-explain paragraph which **either**:

- builds on the paragraph above, looking at how Orwell creates a disturbing mood **or**
- explores how Orwell creates the mood which you identified in Activity 1 on page 81.

IMPROVING YOUR LEVEL

Level 3	Level 4	Level 5	Level 6
Identify the mood the writer has tried to create	Identify and make some undeveloped comments on the mood the writer has tried to create	Explain how the writer's choice of detail and language helps create mood	Explore how the writer's choice of detail and language contributes to the mood of the text as a whole, and its likely effect on the reader

REMEMBER

- **Identify** the atmosphere or mood which the writer creates.
- **Explain** which details the writer uses to create the mood.
- **Explore** how the writer has selected the language of these details to create the mood.

5.4 Character

What am I learning?

You are learning how writers use language to create characters.

Characters are one of the most important parts of any story. If we are interested in the characters, we will care what happens to them and keep reading or watching.

Identify what a character is like.

ACTIVITY 1

1 Read the extract from Willy Russell's play, *Educating Rita* on the opposite page.

Rita is a hairdresser from Liverpool who wants to be a student and learn about English literature. She has come to meet Frank, a university lecturer. He is in his office, on the telephone to his partner, Julia. Rita has knocked on his door.

There is another knock at the door

FRANK: *(Calling in the direction of the door)* Come in! *(He continues on the telephone)* Yes ... All right ... yes ... Bye, bye ... *(He replaces the receiver)* Yes, that's it, you just pop off and put your head in the oven. *(Shouting)* Come in! Come in!

RITA: *(from the doorway)* I'm comin' in, aren't I? It's that stupid bleedin' handle on the door. You wanna get it fixed. *(She comes into the room.)*

FRANK: *(staring, slightly confused)* Erm – yes, I suppose I always mean to...

RITA: *(going to the chair by the desk and dumping her bag)* Well that's no good always meaning to, is it? Y'should get on with it; one of these days you'll be shoutin' 'Come in' an' it'll go on forever because the poor sod on the other side won't be able to get in. An' you won't be able to get out.

FRANK stares at RITA who stands by the desk.

2 Choose two of the words below and one of your own to describe the characters of:

a Frank **b** Rita

angry   cheeky   rude   amusing

uncaring   confrontational   aggressive   confused   disrespectful

Explain how the writer has used language to create a character.

ACTIVITY 2

1 Once you have decided what a character is 'like', you need to find the evidence from the text which suggested this to you. Look at what the character **says** and **does**.

For example, if you decided that Willy Russell wanted to suggest that Frank was **uncaring**...

...you might choose this quote to prove it:

You can then explain how **what the character says** suggested this to you...

...and then how **what the character does** suggested this to you.

> When Frank finishes his phone call to his partner, Julia, the writer suggests that he is uncaring:
>
> '(He replaces the receiver) Yes, that's it, you just pop off and put your head in the oven.'
>
>   He is saying that he wishes his partner would kill herself, which suggests that he does not have a very good relationship with her.
>   He says this after he has put the phone down so she cannot hear him. This could suggest that he does not really mean it – or that he is too cowardly to say it directly to her.

2 Identify evidence from the text on page 84 to prove:

   a your answers from Activity 1 – what Frank is like

   b your answers from Activity 1 – what Rita is like.

3 For each piece of evidence, write a sentence or two explaining what these quotes suggest to you by looking at what the character says, and/or what the character does.

Explore closely the language which the writer has given to the characters.

ACTIVITY 3

1 Look closely at the language in the extract which the writer has given to Rita. The writer has created patterns and connections in the way in which Rita speaks.

   a What do you notice about the way in which each of these sentences ends? What does this suggest about the character of Rita?

> I'm comin' in, aren't I?

> Well that's no good always meaning to, is it?

   b What do you notice about the language which the writer has given Rita in these two sentences? What does this suggest about the character of Rita?

> It's that stupid bleedin' handle on the door.

> the poor sod on the other side won't be able to get in.

   c What do you notice about the language which the writer has given Rita in these two sentences? What does this suggest about the character of Rita?

> You wanna get it fixed.

> Y'should get on with it

   d The writer has used a lot of apostrophes to show the way in which Rita pronounces her words. What does this suggest to you about the character of Rita?

> one of these days you'll be shoutin' 'Come in' an' it'll go on forever

2 Write a point-evidence-explain paragraph about the character of Rita. Follow these guidelines:

In your **point:**   describe Rita's character.

In your **evidence**: choose a quote which demonstrates her character and the writer's choice of language.

To **explain:**   make at least **two** comments on different aspects of her language and what they suggest about her character.

make at least **one** comment about what she does and what it suggests about her character.

IMPROVING YOUR LEVEL

Level 3	Level 4	Level 5	Level 6
Identify the nature of a character in a text	Identify and make some undeveloped comments on the nature of a character in a text	Explain how the writer's choice of language has contributed to the presentation of character	Explore how the writer's choice of language, particularly in its patterns and connections, contributes to the character as a whole, and its likely effect on the reader

REMEMBER

- **Identify** what a character is like.
- **Explain** what a character is like, using evidence to comment on what they say and do.
- **Explore** how the writer has created connections and patterns in the character's language.

5.5 Language and audience

What am I learning?

You are learning how writers select language appropriate to their audience.

A writer's choice of language often depends on the audience (the readers) for which they are writing. The audience is usually described by their age and/or gender.

Identify the intended audience for a text.

ACTIVITY 1

1 Look at extracts A and B below and opposite from the Cafcass website. They give information to support people whose families are having problems.

A

INFO FOR TEENAGERS

Sometimes families experience problems. Your parents or carers might be splitting up, or they might be finding it difficult to look after you properly. Families can usually sort out these problems, but sometimes they can't. Specially trained people such as solicitors, judges, magistrates or social workers may need to get involved in sorting out the situation.

That's when a family court can help with big decisions, like who you should live with and who you should see. The aim is for everyone to agree, but if that's not possible, a judge or magistrate will look at all the facts and help make the best decision possible.

B

INFO FOR FAMILIES

If parents or carers separate or divorce, and can't agree on arrangements for their children, they may refer their dispute to a family court to make a decision. Most court cases concerning children involve private disputes between parents about the issues of residence and contact.

Although people still commonly speak about 'custody' and 'access' these terms were abolished by the Children Act 1989 ... The concepts of parental responsibility and residence replaced 'custody'... The term contact replaces the previous term 'access'.

2 Who is the audience for Text A?

3 Who is the audience for Text B?

Explain how the writer's language choice is appropriate to the audience.

ACTIVITY 2

1 A lot of the information given in these two web pages is the same. Look at these sentences. One is taken from Text A, the other from Text B.

Text A

Your parents or carers might be splitting up, or they might be finding it difficult to look after you properly. Families can usually sort out these problems, but sometimes they can't.

Text B

If parents or carers separate or divorce, and can't agree on arrangements for their children, they may refer their dispute to a family court to make a decision.

What's the connection between the two pairs of circled words?

2 Which of the four circled words would you describe as:

a formal   c simple
b informal   d complex?

3   In what ways is the writer's language choice in the two texts on pages 88 and 89 appropriate to their intended audiences? Write a sentence or two explaining each of your answers, for example:

> In Text A, the writer selects language which is _____ and _____. The intended audience for this text is _____. The language is appropriate for this audience because...

Explore how the writer's language choice creates an appropriate tone.

ACTIVITY 3

1   Text A frequently uses the words *you* and *your*. It talks to or *addresses* the reader directly. Why might this be appropriate to its audience?

2   Text A uses positive language to explain what happens when families have problems:

> best decision possible

> sorting out the situation

How would you describe the tone that this gives the text? Put these possible answers in order – the one you agree with most at the top and the one you agree with least at the bottom:

> **tone:** like *mood*, the kind of 'voice' in which the text is written

*   positive
*   happy
*   comforting
*   reassuring
*   friendly

3   Text B does not directly address the reader. It uses complex, formal language which is neither positive nor negative. How would you describe the tone that this gives the text? Put these possible answers in order:

*   serious
*   balanced
*   knowledgeable
*   unemotional
*   depressing

4 Look at this point-evidence-explain paragraph. It comments on the tone of Text A.

point

evidence

explain

> The intended audience for Text A is young people:
> 'That's when a family court can help with big decisions,
> like who you should live with and who you should see.'
> The writer has chosen simple vocabulary such as 'who
> you should live with' so that young people can easily
> understand the decisions which a family court will help
> make. The text addresses the reader directly ('you')
> and uses positive language ('big decisions') to create
> a friendly and reassuring tone.

Explain how the language – formal or informal, complex or simple – is appropriate to the audience.

What tone has the writer created? How?

Comment on specific words from the evidence.

Using the example above, write a similar paragraph commenting on the tone of Text B. Use labels and arrows to show the different features you have included in your paragraph.

IMPROVING YOUR LEVEL

Level 3	Level 4	Level 5	Level 6
Identify a text's intended audience	Identify a text's intended audience and make some undeveloped comments on how the writer's choice of language is appropriate to it	Explain how the writer's choice of language is appropriate to its audience, eg more formal complex language for adults	Explore how the writer's choice of language creates a tone which is appropriate to a text's intended audience

REMEMBER

- **Identify** the audience at which the writer is aiming.
- **Explain** how the writer has selected language which is appropriate to that audience.
- **Explore** how the writer's language choices creates a tone appropriate to that audience.

5.6 Rhetorical devices in narrative writing

What am I learning?

You are learning how writers select language features to create specific effects.

As well as particular words, writers often select language techniques or **rhetorical devices** to emphasise a particular idea or effect and make the reader respond in the way they want.

Identify the rhetorical devices which the writer has chosen to use.

ACTIVITY 1

1 Look at the rhetorical devices on the left below. Match each one to the correct definition on the right.

contrast	Repeating a word or phrase to emphasise an idea.
repetition	Positioning two opposing, very different things or ideas next to each other to emphasise their difference.
list	A word or phrase intended to create an emotional reaction in the reader, for example, sadness, joy, horror, anger, sympathy, etc.
short sentence	A series of related objects or ideas, separated by commas, to emphasise their breadth or range.
emotive language	A sentence of around five words or fewer, used for dramatic impact. Sometimes used after a longer sentence to exaggerate the effect.

2 Look at the five short extracts below. Each one demonstrates at least one of the rhetorical devices you identified in question 1.

A A shaft of white light pierced the blackness.

B He gave her chocolates, he gave her flowers, he gave her presents every day.

C He stuffed himself with sausages, bacon, eggs, beans, mushrooms, fried bread, toast, butter and jam.

D He looked into the distance, listened to the silence for several minutes, but there was nothing. He was alone.

E The creature slaughtered every living thing in its path.

Identify the rhetorical devices which the writer has used in each of the five extracts.

Explain the effect of rhetorical devices on the reader.

ACTIVITY 2

1 Read the following extract from Chapter 1 of *The Demon Assassin* by Alan Gibbons.

> Paul isn't there. The instant Mum sees his room is empty her heart stutters. The PC, usually left on twenty-four-seven, is switched off. There's none of Paul's usual clutter on the floor or on the table: no discarded clothes, no books lying face down on the desk, no DVDs or computer games. For once, everything is neatly filed away. He's even made the bed. The whole place has the appearance of a hotel bedroom.
>
> 'Paul,' she cries, knowing there's no point, 'Paul!'
>
> Paul's girlfriend Netty hovers behind the distraught Mrs Rector, feeling like an intruder on a mother's grief. Mum grabs the phone and calls him. She gets a recorded message: the number you have called is unavailable.

2 In the extract, the writer has used each of the five rhetorical devices which you identified in Activity 1. Choose a quotation to show where the writer has used each one, and write a sentence or two explaining its effect, using the definitions in Activity 1 to help you. Write your answers in a table like the one below. The first one has been done to help you.

Rhetorical device	Quotation	Effect
Contrast	'There's none of Paul's usual clutter on the floor... For once, everything is neatly filed away.'	The contrast between what Mum expects and what she finds emphasises that something is wrong.
Repetition		

93

Explore how rhetorical devices contribute to the overall effect of the text.

ACTIVITY 3

1 To explore a text effectively you need to:

Look at its overall effect …

… and coment on how the writer's choice of language contributes to it.

a Which **three** of these statements about the opening of *The Demon Assassin* do you most agree with? Make sure you have evidence to prove your decision.

- Paul has disappeared.
- Mum is upset.
- Paul has run away from home.
- Paul has been kidnapped.
- Something dramatic and strange has happened.

b Look at your answers to Activity 2 on page 93. Can you connect any of the rhetorical devices and their effect to the statements you selected in question 1a? One has been done to help you.

- contrast
- repetition
- list
- short sentence
- emotive language

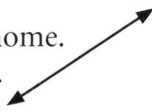

2 Look at this point-evidence-explain paragraph. It comments on how the writer's use of contrast contributes to the overall effect of the text.

point —

evidence —

explain —

Paul has disappeared from home, leaving his bedroom neat and tidy.

'There's none of Paul's usual clutter on the floor... For once, everything is neatly filed away.'

The writer is suggesting that something strange and dramatic has happened to Paul. The writer emphasises this by contrasting what Mum usually expects to find in his room with what she actually finds.

Explain the overall effect of the text – see your answers to question 1 on page 94.

Explore how the writer's use of a rhetorical device contributes to the overall effect – see your answers to Activity 2 on page 93.

3 Write point-evidence-explain paragraphs about the other two statements you selected in question 1a page 94. Remember to connect the writer's use of rhetorical devices to the overall effect.

IMPROVING YOUR LEVEL

Level 3	Level 4	Level 5	Level 6
Identify one or two rhetorical devices which a writer has used	Identify a range of rhetorical devices which a writer has used and make undeveloped comments on their effect	Explain the likely effect of a range of rhetorical devices on the reader	Explore how the writer's choice of a range of rhetorical devices contributes to the effect of the text on the reader as a whole

REMEMBER

- **Identify** the rhetorical devices which the writer has chosen to use.
- **Explain** the effect of the writer's choice of rhetorical devices.
- **Explore** the effect of the whole text and how the writer's choice of rhetorical devices contributes to it.

5.7 Rhetorical devices in non-fiction and media texts

What am I learning?

You are learning how writers select language features to create specific effects.

Writers of non-fiction texts often use rhetorical devices – particularly when writing to argue or persuade – to influence their readers' actions and opinions.

Identify the rhetorical devices which the writer has chosen to use.

ACTIVITY 1

1 Read this text. It is taken from a cereal packet.

> **BodyGood Oats** are packed with enough nutritious goodness to set you up for the whole day. Enjoy them with milk, or top them off with some banana for a quick, healthy and satisfying kickstart.
>
> In fact, **BodyGood** Oats are so good, why not enjoy them any time? Try **BodyGood Oats** with hot milk and a drizzle of honey for a warming winter night-time treat. Or you can go for a tropical summer tea-time snack by adding a tasty sprinkling of dried fruit and coconut.
>
> **Delicious!**

2 How many of the rhetorical devices defined below can you identify in the text?

Rhetorical device bingo!		
Rhetorical question A question which does not need, or suggests its own, answer to involve the reader, for example, *Why do we bother?*	**Positive *or* negative language** Descriptive language to emphasise good or bad qualities, for example, *superb* or *appalling*.	**Call to action** The writer suggests that doing as they say will bring positive results, for example, *Do it today and your life will be 100% better.*
Pattern of three A cluster of three related words or phrases to emphasise the writer's point, for example, *Cool, fruity and refreshing.*	**Imperative *or* command** A verb which gives the reader an order, for example, *Enjoy yourself!*	**Direct address** The writer talks directly to the reader to draw them in to the argument, for example, *you/your* or *we/our.*

Explain the effect of rhetorical devices on the reader.

ACTIVITY 2

1 Read the newspaper article below.

Don't let girls grow up too quickly

A study courtesy of the Girl Guides proves what we have long suspected: girls as young as 10 are under colossal pressure to grow up and are buckling under the strain.

Appearing fit, healthy and fizzing with youthful energy will no longer suffice. Barely even into their teens, girls are being made to feel failures if they are not slim, sexy and as glamorous as the far older women they gaze at in magazines.

… may I remind you that it wasn't always thus? Girls have always cared about the way they looked. The difference is, growing up in the Sixties, Seventies and Eighties, we girls cared passionately about a host of other things, too.

Parents made sure not to compliment particularly good-looking children, 'so as not to give her a big head'. Spending too long gazing at one's reflection in the mirror was not praised but frowned upon. Far from being encouraged to look glamorous, … girls were expected to look 'nice'. Nice meant clean and tidy with brushed hair, scrubbed cheeks and bright, sparkling eyes. It most definitely did not mean plastered in fake tan, with a head full of acrylic hair extensions, false nails and a tattooed lipstick line …

It's high time we reassessed our priorities … and allowed our little girls to relax and concentrate on being children.

From the *Daily Express*, July 2008

2 Answer these questions to sum up the writer's key points.

  a What does the writer think is the main problem facing girls today?
  b How does the writer think life is different for girls today compared to the 1980s and earlier?
  c Look at these words from the text:

  slim   glamorous

Does the writer think these are positive qualities? Write a sentence explaining your answer.

3 Look at the table below. It identifies six rhetorical devices which the writer has used in the article on page 97. Look at the rhetorical devices decribed on page 96 to help you.

   a Find an example of each rhetorical device in the text on page 97.
   b Write a sentence or two explaining the effect the writer wants each rhetorical device to have on the reader.

Rhetorical device	Example	Explanation
Positive language	'fit, healthy'	The writer wants the reader to agree that these are positive qualities which should be encouraged in girls.
Negative language		
Rhetorical question		
Pattern of three		
Contrast		
List		

Explore which rhetorical devices make the greatest persuasive contribution.

ACTIVITY 3

1 Texts often use a wide range of rhetorical devices. It is important that you select and write about those which make a significant contribution to the overall effect of the text.

   a Look again at your answers to question 3 above. Which **three** of these rhetorical devices do you think are the most effective in making the writer's point of view persuasive?
   b Write a sentence or two explaining:
     i why you selected each rhetorical device, for example:

> The use of negative language, for example, 'colossal pressure' and 'failure', highlights how important the writer feels this problem is for young girls.

     ii how each device you selected supports and emphasises the key points you noted in question 3, for example:

> The writer uses negative language to describe every aspect of the key issue in her argument: the negative pressure girls are under and the negative effect this has on them.

IMPROVING YOUR LEVEL

Level 3	Level 4	Level 5	Level 6
Identify one or two rhetorical devices which a writer has used	Identify a range of rhetorical devices which a writer has used and make undeveloped comments on their effect	Explain the likely effect of a range of rhetorical devices on the reader	Explore how the writer's choice of a range of rhetorical devices contributes to the effect of the text on the reader as a whole

REMEMBER

- **Identify** the rhetorical devices which the writer has chosen to use.
- **Explain** the effect of rhetorical devices on the reader.
- **Explore** the most significant rhetorical devices and their contribution to the overall effect of the text.

5.8 Literary features

What am I learning?

You are learning how writers use literary features to create an impact on the reader.

Writers choose words and phrases for their meaning, their connotations, for the images they create in the reader's imagination and, sometimes, their sound.

Identify the literary features which the writer has chosen to use.

ACTIVITY 1

Definitions of literary features

Rhyme: when two words have endings with a similar sound.

Alliteration: two or more words, near or next to each other, beginning with the same letter or sound. For example: his shoes scuffed through the snow.

Onomatopoeia: a word whose sound imitates its meaning. For example: Bang!

Simile: a comparison of two different things, using *like* or *as*. For example: he towered over me like a skyscraper, as tall as the sky.

Metaphor: a *direct* comparison of two different things, without the use of *like* or *as*. For example: he was a skyscraper.

Personification: a kind of metaphor, describing a non-human object as if it were a person. For example: the trees groaned in the wind.

1 Literary features are often found in literature – fiction, poetry and drama – but also in non-fiction, for example, newspaper headlines. Look at the texts opposite.

Tea leaf stops crazed thief

A woman and her baby escaped unhurt after calming a burglar down with a cup of tea.

BRITISH ECONOMY ON THE BRINK

BRITAIN is only three months away from recession.

Which literary features can you identify in these newspaper headlines?

2 Read this extract from a poem called *Colin Clouts Come Home Againe*, written by Edmund Spenser in 1595.

> So to the sea we came; the sea, that is
> A world of waters heaped up on high,
> Rolling like mountains in wild wilderness,
> Horrible, hideous, roaring with hoarse cry.

Adapted from original poem

a What is the poet describing in this verse?

b Which literary features can you identify in the poem extract?

Explain the effect on the reader of the literary features the writer has chosen to use.

ACTIVITY 2

1 Trace the path of each literary feature, through its purpose, to one or more of the effects which you think it can create. One has been done to get you started.

Literary feature	Purpose	Effect
Rhyme	To engage the reader's ear	It makes the writing appealing and memorable.
Alliteration		It creates a vivid visual image.
Onomatopoeia		It surprises the reader into seeing in a different way.
Simile	To engage the reader's imagination	It adds punch and emphasis to the writing.
Metaphor		It builds the description with new ideas and connotations.
Personification		It helps the writer describe what you can hear and see.

2 **a** Why do newspapers give their articles headlines?

    b Write two or three sentences explaining the effect of literary features in headlines, using one of the examples on page 101 as evidence

3 Look again at the poem extract on page 101. Select at least one example of a literary feature which the poet has chosen to use. Write two or three sentences explaining its effect.

Explore the cumulative effect of the poet's choice of language.

ACTIVITY 3

1 Look again at the words which the poet has chosen to use on page 139.

a   came   cry   heaped   hideous   high   hoarse   horrible   in   is   like   mountains   of   on   roaring   rolling   sea   up   waters   so   that   the   we   wild   to   with   world   wilderness

    a Choose **one** word from the poem that you think best sums up the key image which the poet is trying to give the reader.

    b Choose **one** literary feature which you think makes an important contribution to this image.

    c Write a point-evidence-explain paragraph exploring the contribution of this literary feature to the key image. You can use this paragraph as a model for your own.

point	The poet describes the sea as [key image] : — Use your answer to 1a here.
evidence	' [quotation] '
explain	The writer is using [literary feature] to suggest that — Use your answer to 1b here. [effect of literary feature] .

IMPROVING YOUR LEVEL

Level 3	Level 4	Level 5	Level 6
Identify one or two examples of figurative language, eg simile	Identify a range of literary features which a writer has used and make undeveloped comments on their effect	Explain the likely effect of a range of literary features on the reader	Explore the cumulative effect of two or more literary features which the writer has chosen to use

REMEMBER

- **Identify** the literary features which the writer has chosen to use.
- **Explain** the effect of the writer's choice of literary features on the reader.
- **Explore** the cumulative effect of the writer's choice of language.

LANGUAGE

AF5 Sample Answers: Levels 3–6

The text

Read the opening of *Star Crossed* by Rachel Wing.

'If this lesson doesn't end soon, I will be forced to jump out of the window to see if I can fly for my own amusement...'

You slide down your seat and even further in your typical Monday-morning state: falling asleep in the cosy atmosphere of the English room, listening to your teacher stammer in that annoying way that she does when she's going on about some great work of English literature or something, written by someone important. Not that you care. A turn of your head lets you look at the clock. 10.15a.m. You sigh and grab your bag from under the desk, shoving the books back into it that you haven't bothered to write in. Miss Phillips is still trying to mutter on in her tiny voice above the noise the class is making. You feel a little stab of pity for your short, wiry teacher as she tries to regain the grumbling class's attention.

The question

Identify the key words in the question.

What does the writer's choice of language suggest about the character of the narrator? You should comment on:
- the narrator's attitude to school
- the narrator's description of her teacher.

Identify the Assessment Focus which the question is asking you about.

Reading Assessment Focus 5:

Explaining and commenting on a writer's use of language, for example:
- How a word or phrase affects the reader's response to an event or character.
- Figurative language: simile, metaphor, personification.
- Patterns or structures in the writer's choice of language.
- Differences in language use, for example, between two characters or narrators.

Level 3

- Sometimes I can identify a word or phrase which the writer has chosen for a reason.
- Sometimes I can explain why the writer has chosen to do this.

I don't think the narrator likes school very much. The narrator hasn't bothered to write in her books so she has not done any work for the whole lesson. The narrator says the teacher is annoying and the class don't listen to her.

> Some relevant details are selected from the text.

> A good point but it is not used to answer the question about the **character of the narrator**.

Level 4

- I can identify some of the choices the writer has made in the language they have used.
- I can usually think of a reason why the writer has made those choices.

At the start of the passage the narrator says she wants the lesson to end soon and she is falling asleep so it doesn't sound like she's very interested in the lesson. This tells me that the lesson is boring or that the narrator is not very interested in school. She also says 'not that you care' so I think the writer wants us to think that the narrator has a negative attitude to school.

> Identifies words and phrases which the writer has used to tell us about the character of the narrator.

> Uses these details to answer the question.

> Gives a reason why the writer made these choices.

Level 5

- I can identify a range of different language features which the writer has chosen to use.
- I can explain why the writer has made these choices.
- I can sometimes comment on the effect of the writer's language choice on the reader.

> The writer suggests that the narrator does not have a very good attitude to school. 'You sigh and grab your bag from under the desk, shoving the books back into it that you haven't bothered to write in.' This suggests that the narrator has not done any work in the lesson and the word 'bothered' suggests it was because the narrator was too lazy or bored to do what she was meant to do.

Uses:
- point
- evidence
- explain

to identify and explain the writer's choices.

Identifies one specific word which the writer has chosen and makes a comment on its effect.

Adding one or two sentences to your answer **can** improve the level.

Level 6

- I can recognise and name a range of different language features.
- I can explain and comment in detail on the effect the writer's language choice has created.
- Sometimes I can see a pattern in the writer's choice of language in a text and comment on why the writer has chosen to do this.

> Also, because the narrator is described as 'shoving' her books into her bag, it suggests that she has no interest in or respect for her school work. All the writer's language choices in this quote and the whole passage are very negative: 'sigh', 'grab', 'shove', 'bothered' suggesting that the narrator has no positive thoughts or feelings about school.

Adds an additional, detailed comment on the writer's choice of language.

Identifies a pattern in the writer's choice of language and its effect.

AF6 PURPOSE AND VIEWPOINT

6.1 Purpose

What am I learning?

You are learning that writers write a text for a purpose, to express a viewpoint.

As a **writer**, you choose the ideas and information which will help your piece of writing do the job you need it to do. As a **reader** you need to be able to work out the writer's purpose and viewpoint and to explore their effect.

Identify the purpose of a text.

ACTIVITY 1

1 Look at the four examples of everyday writing below and on the following page.

A

> Manisha has worked hard in English this year. She reads carefully and fluently, often reading between the lines to identify the writer's point of view in a range of texts. Manisha should continue her personal reading in order to further develop.

B

> Video games will be forced to carry cigarette-style health warnings under proposals to protect children from unsuitable digital material. The report, commissioned by the Prime Minister in response …

C

With wonderful sea views and a short walk to the beach, this is the perfect hotel for a relaxing family break. With two kids' pools and a VIP jacuzzi area, it means luxury for you and fun for the kids.

D

Press any button to turn on your MPLAY3. The main menu appears. You can use the up (↑) and down (↓) arrows and the Select button to navigate through onscreen menus, play songs and change settings.

2 Complete the table below identifying the purpose of the different texts on pages 107–108. Use the purpose bank to help you. The first one has been done for you.

Purpose bank

imagine	entertain	explore
inform	explain	describe
argue	persuade	advise
analyse	comment	review

Writing example	Why did the writer write it?	Purpose	How I know
1 School report	To tell Manisha and her parents about her progress in English lessons.	Inform/advise	The report says what Manisha has done (inform) and what she should do in the future (advise).
2 Newspaper article			
3 Instruction manual			
4 Holiday brochure			

3 Choose **three** more examples of everyday texts from the list below:

- Leaflet from your local pizza delivery service
- A TV guide magazine
- A children's story book
- Your most recent history essay
- The last text message you sent.

Add them to your table.

Explain the purpose of a text.

ACTIVITY 2

1 In question 1 on page 107, you read the start of a newspaper article. Now read the complete article.

Computer games to get health warnings

1 Video games will be forced to carry cigarette-style health warnings under proposals to protect children from unsuitable digital material.

2 The report, commissioned by the Prime Minister in response to a growing moral panic about video games, will conclude that they can harm the development of children's beliefs and values and desensitise them to violence. It will also recommend that retailers who sell video games to anyone under the age rating on the box should face a hefty fine or up to five years in prison, *The Times* has learnt.

3 The report, written by Tanya Byron, the clinical psychologist and television parenting guru, is also expected to address the dangers of children's use of the internet.

4 'Parents are afraid to let their children out,' she said. 'So they keep them at home, but allow them to take risks online.'

5 She will call for a massive campaign to educate parents, teachers and childcarers about how to ensure that children get maximum benefit from the digital world without being exposed to its dangers.

6 This will include a drive for greater awareness of inappropriate content such as pornography. Parents will be encouraged to monitor children's online use and keep computers in living rooms rather than bedrooms. Dr Byron said that video and online games could have enormous benefits 'in terms of learning and development', but that there was too little awareness among parents about the associated risks they posed and how to manage those risks.

7 'You would not send your child to the pool without teaching them to swim, so why would you let them online without teaching them to manage the risks?' she said.

8 Dr Byron said that the current classification system for video games was confusing and not tough enough … Dr Byron wants a single statutory classification system. Ratings would have to be displayed prominently on all packaging materials, like health warnings on cigarettes, as well as on shop display cases … She also wants all games consoles to contain blocking mechanisms that would enable parents to prevent children playing unsuitable games on them.

From *The Times*, March 27th 2008

2 The article on page 109 has eight paragraphs. Each of the **first four** paragraphs could be summed up as one of these key points:

> A The report comments on children's use of the internet.
> B A report has warned that video games can have a negative effect on children.
> C The report's writer feels that parents should be more concerned about their children's Internet use.
> D 'Health' warnings are going to appear on video games

Which of the first four paragraphs matches with which key point?

3 Now look at the **last** four paragraphs of the article. Write a sentence or two summing up the key point of each of these paragraphs.

4 Look again at the eight key points you have identified from the article. Which are the two or three most important key points? Use them to write your own summary of the article in approximately 20 words.

5 a Who wrote this newspaper article?
  b Does the writer express her own point of view?
  c Why do you think this is?

Explore the purpose of a text.

ACTIVITY 3

1 Read these notes made by a student who explored the news article on page 109.

The report says:
A video games should carry health warnings to protect children
B games can harm children
C retailers who sell video games to anyone under the age rating on the box should be fined or go to prison
D the report will warn about the dangers of children's use of the internet
E parents, teachers and childcarers should be taught how to ensure that children benefit from the Internet without being exposed to its dangers
F parents will be encouraged to monitor children's online use
G parents are not aware of the risks of computer games
H the current classification system for video games is confusing and not tough enough
I there should be one, clear rating system for video games
J ratings will have to be displayed on all packaging and on shop display cases
K games consoles should contain blocking mechanisms so parents can prevent children playing unsuitable games.

Decide which of these points could be organised under the headings in the table below. Then copy and complete the table. Some have been done for you.

The problem	What parents should do	How video game companies will be affected	How retailers will be affected
B, D, E	F		

2 Use these notes to write a paragraph that explores the purposes of the report. You could use the sentence starters below to help you:

This newspaper article has been written to...

A report has found that the problem is...

The report makes several recommendations. It suggests that parents should...

It also suggests that video game companies should...

Finally, it suggests that retailers should...

The writer of the newspaper article's opinion is...

IMPROVING YOUR LEVEL

Level 3	Level 4	Level 5	Level 6
Identify the purpose of a text	Identify the purpose of a range of texts and the key features that identified it	Identify and explain the purpose and key points of a text	Explore how the key points of a text contribute to its overall purpose

REMEMBER

- Identify the purpose of the text.
- Explain the purpose of a text by identifying key points.
- Explore the purpose of a text by making connections between key points.

6.2 Viewpoint

What am I learning?

You are learning that a text can express a writer's viewpoint.

When you are looking at a view, your viewpoint will affect what you can see. It may give you an overview, a partial view or even no view at all! When you are exploring a text, your viewpoint will affect what you think and feel.

Identify the writer's viewpoint.

ACTIVITY 1

1 a Look at this selection of texts in which the writer is expressing a point of view.

A

Reviews: *The Dark Knight*

Superb special effects and gadgets grab the eye, as always. Watch out for Batman's 'new look' sexy suit, and as always his transportation rocks! A word of warning though – close your eyes if the Joker's about – he kills in the most revolting ways!

In short, it's a great work out for the mind and your adrenalin will flow. Don't miss it!

B

…Fox hunting originated in the United Kingdom in the 16th century, but is practised all over the world… The sport is controversial, particularly in the UK, where a ban was introduced in November 2004. Proponents see it as an important part of rural culture, vital for conservation and pest control, while opponents argue that it is cruel and unnecessary…

C

Letters Page

The canals and rivers in our towns and cities are being ruined by abandoned supermarket trollies. It must be extremely expensive for the supermarkets to replace them and, no doubt, this expense is passed onto shoppers at the checkouts. Worse still, our canals are beginning to look more like trolley graveyards than havens of wildlife.

Here are some words which can be used to sum up a writer's viewpoint:

positive   negative   objective

b How would you describe the writer's point of view in each of these three texts?

objective: a neutral, unbiased point of view

Explain how a writer shows the reader their viewpoint.

ACTIVITY 2

1 a Look again at any of the texts in question 1 in which you felt the writer presents a **positive** point of view. Identify at least two words or phrases from each text which suggest this.

b Look again at any of the texts in question 1 in which you felt the writer presents a **negative** point of view. Identify at least two words or phrases from each text which suggest this.

c Look again at any of the texts in question 1 in which you felt the writer presents an **objective** point of view. How has the writer achieved this?

Explore how a writer shows the reader their viewpoint.

ACTIVITY 3

Sometimes a writer's viewpoint is more complex than simply positive or negative.

1 Read the following extract (on page 114) taken from Helen Sharman's autobiography *Seize the Moment*. Helen is an astronaut and this is an account of her first space flight.

In my earphones, a voice from the bunker said, 'Five minutes to go. Please close the masks of your helmets.'

The three of us obeyed, then confirmed. … The bunker replied, 'Everything on board is correct and we are now ready to launch.'

A little later, the voice said, 'Two minutes.' Then it said 'One minute.'

Now that we were not moving around or reaching for the controls above us, it was comfortable to be sitting there in the spacesuit. … I felt the pressure of Tolya's elbow against mine. I could hear the quiet hiss of static in the speaker against my ear. Sergei said nothing, Tolya said nothing; the voice from the bunker was silent. It was a moment of stillness, of final waiting. My feet were still cold.

Far away, deep below, there came a rumbling noise as the rocket engines ignited. On the control panel, the on-board clock had started automatically; we were nominally one second into the mission, then two, and the engines still rumbled far below. Three seconds and the rumbling grew louder and, as the four launch-gantries swung away, I could feel vibration but no sense of acceleration. … But the engines continued to roar beneath us and the instruments confirmed that we were away from the tower, that acceleration was beginning to build, and we could feel the pressure of g-forces growing steadily against us.

2 a How would you describe Helen Sharman's viewpoint in this extract? Choose one or more of the following – or use your own ideas.

> anxious   excited   frightened   bored

b For each word you chose, select a quotation to support your answer.

c Look closely at each quotation you have selected. Which techniques has Sharman used in order to suggest her viewpoint? What effect do they have? Use this table to help you:

Technique	Effect
descriptive language	to help the reader imagine the experience
counting time	to build tension
short sentences	to create drama
repetition	to emphasise a point or idea
using the five senses	to show how her experience looked, sounded, felt, etc.

d Use your answers to questions 2a–c to help you write a point-evidence-explanation paragraph, exploring Sharman's viewpoint in this extract. You can use the following sentence starters to help you.

point — In this extract, Sharman's viewpoint suggests she is... _____ :

Use your answer to question 2a here.

evidence — ' _____ [quotation] _____ '

Use your answer to question 2b here.

explain — Sharman uses technique to suggest that effect...

Use your answer to question 2c here.

IMPROVING YOUR LEVEL

Level 3	Level 4	Level 5	Level 6
Identify the writer's viewpoint	Identify and make some comment on the writer's viewpoint, eg positive or negative	Explain how the writer's choice of key points and language helps get their viewpoint across to the reader	Explore the writer's choice of key points and language to comment on their viewpoint in more detail

REMEMBER

- **Identify** the writer's point of view.
- **Explain** how the writer's language choice creates this point of view.
- **Explore** a range of techniques the writer uses to express their point of view.

6.3 Narrative viewpoint

What am I learning?

You are learning how writers tell stories from different viewpoints and the effect this can have.

The narrator in a story is the voice which the writer uses in order to tell the tale. Sometimes writers tell stories in their own voices and sometimes they write as if they are one of the characters in the story.

Identify the narrative viewpoint.

ACTIVITY 1

When a writer writes a text, they can place themselves in the text by writing in the **first person** or they can present themselves as a more objective voice by writing in the **third person**.

Some stories are told in the first person. Some stories are told in the third person.

> **first person:** the writer's voice speaks directly to you. This is common in newspaper articles where the journalist gives you their opinion, and in autobiographies, letters and diaries. The writer often uses 'I' or 'we'
>
> **third person:** the writer does not use 'I', but refers to the characters or people involved as 'he', 'she' or 'they'. This is common in news stories and textbooks

1 a Read these two extracts, taken from the openings of stories:

A

> **King**
> For this story to make any sense, you've got to understand what Simon Waites was like. Thing is, Waitesy never *ever* done nothing wrong. If the lot of us wagged Worzel's lesson, he'd still go on his own. And if we all had Harjit thinking the Head was after him, Waitesy'd let on without a *second thought*.

From *King* by Jon Blake

B

Steel Trapp

Kyle Trapp's heart soared. He loved flying, and he was currently piloting a single-engine Cessna two thousand metres above Lake Michigan. The sky shone blue above lake water of cinnamon grey. Kyle possessed information vital to the investigation, a secret so sensitive that he couldn't trust telephones or email; he could deliver it only in person. He checked his watch: another two hours.

From *Steel Trapp* by Ridley Pearson

b In which person are these two extracts narrated – first person or third person?

Explain the effect of the writer's choice of narrative viewpoint.

ACTIVITY 2

1 Text A is the first paragraph of Jon Blake's story, *King*. Read the next few paragraphs.

I don't suppose it's hard to guess how a youth like that got on in our school. He joined just about every club out so he never had to go in the playground. Mummy and Daddy picked him up straight after school, and no one ever saw him till next morning. Half past eight he'd be in, with his little black briefcase full of homework. They must've cropped a forest to find that youth enough paper.

Funny enough though, not all the teachers liked him. They liked the fact he never answered back all right, but they weren't so keen on him following them all about, like a little dog. Hung on every little word they said, he did. Like it was a matter of *life and death*. All a teacher had to do was cough, and he'd try and write it down.

Of course, you don't get the full picture till you know what he looked like. Well, put it this way. If you stuck a pair of wings on him, all he needed was the harp and the little cloud to float around on. He had these two little pudgy cheeks, and this insy red blob of a mouth like a squashed raspberry. Then there was his hair, which was all soft and curly and blonde, like a baby's. Not to mention the legs. PE was nothing without seeing his puny Dulux White sticks. Tarzan, Mr McHugh called him.

2 a Sometimes a writer will take on a **persona**: they will write as if they are someone else. Who do you think is the narrator of this story?

b What do you learn about the character of Simon Waites? Choose two quotations and write a sentence or two explaining what each one suggests about him.

c What do you learn about the character of the narrator in Text A? Choose two quotations and write a sentence or two explaining what each one suggests about him.

d What do you notice about the kind of language which the narrator uses? Why do you think the writer has chosen to write in this way?

e Why do you think the writer might have chosen this narrator for this story?

> **persona**: an alternative identity which a writer uses in a text, but which does not necessarily represent them or their real viewpoint

Explore the effect of the writer's choice of viewpoint.

ACTIVITY 3

1 Look at these statements about the character of Simon Waites:

- He's just a person like everyone else. I feel a bit sorry for him.
- He is a bit strange and I think he's weird. He interests me.
- He is a figure to laugh at and make fun of. I don't feel sorry for him.
- I don't like the way he is. I don't like him.

Which of these statements reflects:

a The narrator of the story's attitude to Simon Waites?

b The writer's attitude to Simon Waites?

c Your attitude to Simon Waites?

d What was the biggest influence on your response to Simon Waites: the narrator's attitude or the writer's attitude?

IMPROVING YOUR LEVEL

Level 3	Level 4	Level 5	Level 6
Identify the narrative viewpoint: 1st or 3rd person	Identify the narrative viewpoint and make some comment on its effect on the reader	Explain how the narrator's viewpoint or the writer's persona might affect the reader's response to a text	Explore the narrator's viewpoint or the writer's persona and distinguish it from the views of the writer

REMEMBER

- **Identify** the narrative viewpoint: first or third person?
- **Explain** how the writer's choice of narrator affects your response to the text.
- **Explore** how the writer's viewpoint may differ from the narrator's.

6.4 Influencing the audience's viewpoint

What am I learning?

You are learning how writers can create a response from an audience.

Everyone reacts differently to a text because we all have our own experiences, ideas and attitudes that affect how we think and feel. Writers try to identify their **audience**, their likely ideas and attitudes, and try to appeal to them in order to achieve their intended purpose.

Identify the writer's intended audience.

> **audience:** a group of people who see or hear a performance; the intended readers of a text

ACTIVITY 1

1 Read this extract from Nigel Hinton's novel, *Buddy*.

Buddy sat down at his desk near the door and noticed that Julius and Charmian weren't in their places behind him. He hoped the twins weren't away. He'd never had black friends before – in fact, he'd said some nasty things to some black kids at his Junior School. But he'd been drawn to Julius and Charmian because they were the only other people who didn't fit in with the rest of the class. He'd started off by admiring the cheerful way they ignored all the spiteful jibes that the other pupils, and even some of the teachers, made. They'd become his allies and then, gradually, his closest friends.

Mr Normington started calling the register. He looked up when there was no answer from Julius and Charmian. 'The Rybeero twins not here? Has anyone seen our coloured cousins?'

'I saw them hanging around the fruit shop after school, yesterday,' Emma Groves said.

There was a ripple of laughter at this old joke. Fruit shop meant bananas. Bananas meant apes. Apes meant Blacks.

Mr Normington pretended innocence. 'Really?' he said. Pause. 'I wonder why?'

Another ripple of conspiratorial laughter. Everyone was happy.

Buddy could have said something. Something angry about how the twins were worth all the rest of the class put together. At the very least he could have sat stony-faced as his friends were mocked. But he smiled. Mr Normington was looking in his direction and, in an attempt to show that he belonged in 3E, and that he was on the side of Mr Normington's bastions and standards, Buddy smiled and joined in the general chuckle.

He hated himself for wanting to belong to all that, but it was true – he did. A huge part of him wanted it.

2 Which audience do you think the writer is aiming this novel at? Children? Adults? Teachers? A different group of people? Write two or three sentences explaining your answer.

Explain the writer's viewpoint and its appeal to an audience.

ACTIVITY 2

1 How did you respond to the characters in the extract? Did you laugh at them, sympathise with them, dislike them, or respond in another way entirely? Write a sentence or two giving your viewpoint on:

a Mr Normington
b Buddy
c Julius and Charmian
d The other students in the class

For each character you write about, use a quotation to help explain your response.

2 How do you think a different reader might respond to the characters in the extract?

a Make a list of three different people who might read this novel - for example, a teenager, a teacher and a parent.
b How might these different readers respond to the characters you wrote about in question 1? Remember to use quotations to help explain your answers.
c Which of these readers' responses do you think is the correct response?

Explore how the writer's viewpoint can influence the reader.

ACTIVITY 3

1 a Writers work very hard to control our response to their texts and make sure that we end up agreeing with their viewpoint. Read 'A Prickly Problem' below. It is a leaflet requesting support for a charity that rescues injured hedgehogs.

A Prickly Problem

Can you spare 25p per week?

That's less than the price of a packet of crisps.
That's less than the price of a soft drink.
That's the cost of keeping me alive for another day.

Send donations to: Heal the Hedgehogs,
PO Box 236,
LONDON, W1

HEAL THE HEDGEHOGS

b What is the purpose of this text?
c What is the writer's viewpoint?
d How has the writer tried to influence the reader's viewpoint? Write two or three sentences commenting on:

  • the slogan
  • the text
  • the images.

e Has the writer influenced your viewpoint? Would you donate money? Write a short paragraph explaining why. Remember to use evidence and explanation to support your answer.

IMPROVING YOUR LEVEL

Level 3	Level 4	Level 5	Level 6
Identify the intended audience of a text	Identify the intended audience of a text and the key features which helped you identify it	Explain the writer's viewpoint and comment on ways in which it might appeal to its intended audience	Explore how the writer tries to influence their audience's viewpoint through their selection of ideas and language

REMEMBER

- **Identify** the writer's intended audience.
- **Explain** your, and the intended audience's, response.
- **Explore** how the writer has tried to influence the reader's viewpoint.

AF6 Sample Answers: Levels 3–6

PURPOSE AND VIEWPOINT

The text

The USA is firmly on the UK's list of top destinations for a great holiday. Every year thousands of British holiday makers flood the airways heading for Florida, California and New York. The theme parks are a big attraction – but there's also great shopping, sunshine and of course 'the sights'– if you don't mind crowds.

So how many of us will be heading for Virginia this summer? Not many – which is precisely why you should give it some serious thought. She has everything and more than you would get from other US destinations, without the hoards of British tourists!

Virginia is a state on the East coast of America (which means shorter journey times and cheaper flights) and she is blessed with hot, hot, hot summers but enough rainfall during the rest of the year to keep her green and heavily forested. With sparkling rivers and tranquil lakes aplenty, and the amazingly abundant Chesapeake Bay coastal region bordering the Atlantic, she can keep the beach and water lovers happy! There are the Blue Ridge Mountains to climb as well, if you have any energy left! The whole state is beautifully maintained and there is an obvious pride in the land and its heritage which shines at every turn.

However, the biggest draw has to be the fantastic array of activities. Virginia boasts over 1000 historical and heritage attractions – it is the site of the first ever settlement by British colonists in the 1600s and the birthplace of the American Revolution (which you and I call the War of Independence). Finally it was also the site for many of the battles in the American Civil War (the Confederate's capital was located in Richmond). Forget dull dry museums and dusty battlefields – Virginia has generously poured funding into re-creations and interactive exhibits; she even has her own colonial village where 200 buildings and costumed actors 'live' 1700s life for all to see (and join in with). She also has her own theme parks – Busch Gardens Europe and Water Country USA – just in case you get withdrawal symptoms!

The question

How does the writer suggest that Virginia would be a good holiday destination?

Identify the key words in the question.

Identify the Assessment Focus that the question is asking you about.

Writing Assessment Focus 6:

Identifying and commenting on writers' purposes and viewpoints, and the overall effect of the text on the reader, for example:
- Presentation of character, incident or ideas.
- Writers' choices in language and structure which reveal viewpoint and influence the reader.
- The moral, point or purpose of a text.
- using a range of punctuation accurately in speech.

Level 3

- I can usually identify what the writer thinks about an incident, character or idea.
- I can say what I think about it.

It's good because its sunny and there's lots to do but some of it's boring like museums. There are theme parks. 'It even has its own theme parks: Busch Gardens Europe and Water Country USA; just in case you get withdrawal symptoms!'

Correctly identifies a simple fact about Virginia and the viewpoint is hinted at by 'its good'.

This answer is very brief and does not cover the full range of material.

Quote not entirely relevant and too long.

Irrelevant personal opinion.

Another simple fact.

Level 4

- I can identify the main purpose of a text.
- I can identify what the writer thinks about an incident, character or idea.
- I can usually explain how I worked out the writer's viewpoint.
- I can usually say what effect the writer's viewpoint has on the reader.

> He says you should go to Virginia because not many people do, so it's less busy and cheaper and it's hot, which British people like because it's cold at home. 'It has everything and more that you would get from other US destinations, without the hoards of British tourists!' He thinks it would be good to visit because there is a lot to do. You can go to the beach and there are theme parks too like Florida.

Point and simple explanation of why this would be appealing to visitors and make it a good destination.

Another attractive feature identified.

Viewpoint understood.

Relevant quotation but not explained.

Point and explanation given.

Level 5

- I can identify what the writer thinks about an incident, character or idea and what they want the reader to think about it.
- I can usually find some evidence to show what the writer has done to get their viewpoint across to the reader.
- I can usually explain how the writer has influenced the reader's viewpoint.

> It's almost as if the writer is in love with this place, the way he calls it 'she'. Then he goes on to describe all the good things about Virginia. We find out about the weather, the land, the sea and the things to do. Even the people are happy and proud to be there, 'there is an obvious pride in the land and its heritage which shines at every turn.' The writer uses positive words like 'sparkling' and 'beautiful'. All of this suggests that people going on holiday to Virginia will love it too.

Answer is focused on viewpoint.

A technique is pointed out and the effect on the reader is suggested.

Explains the effect of all the evidence and how it might influence the reader.

Writer's choice of language is identified.

Evidence is given to support point.

Level 6

- I can work out what the writer thinks about an incident, character or idea based on close analysis of the writer's choice of language.
- I can clearly explain the effect on the reader and comment on how the writer has created it.

It's obvious that the writer thinks Virginia is great. He criticises more popular destinations, 'if you don't mind crowds' to make it look even better because nobody likes crowds. The writer has no negative points about Virginia, he just praises it using words like 'blessed', 'sparkling', 'tranquil', 'amazingly abundant' and 'beautifully maintained.' These words are all positive, suggesting it is beautiful, peaceful and well cared for by the people who live there. This makes us think that it is somewhere worth caring for and that we would admire it too. The writer gives a long list of all the things to see and do: '... sparkling rivers and tranquil lakes ...Chesapeake Bay coastal region ... Blue Ridge Mountains...'. This makes us think that Virginia would be an amazing place to visit which helps the writer persuade us to book a holiday there.

A confident start which shows a clear understanding of viewpoint.

Focus is immediately on a technique that the writer uses, its effect on reader clearly explained.

Close focus on language with comment on its effect on the reader. This would be better done individually.

Uses explanation of point to comment on writer's purpose and viewpoint.

Writer's technique identified, supported with carefully edited evidence.

Reading skills practice

That Awkward Age...

1 One of the happiest sights of last summer was my 14-year-old daughter nose deep in a book for hours on end. She devoured three adult books that week, three more books than she had read in the previous year. I had been worried by how she had suddenly lost interest in reading when she had been passionate about it as a child. Now she was not only reading adult books, we were talking about them.

2 Keeping children reading as teenagers can be almost impossible when the competition from other forms of entertainment is so fierce: mobile phones, computer games, internet chat rooms, music, hundreds of different TV channels, videos and DVDs. And then there's the pressure of work that comes with secondary school. Curling up in bed with a book at the end of a school day is unlikely to feel like a good way of winding down.

3 And as Chris Cross, who at 16 has set up the website Coolreads where teenagers review books, explains: 'There has always been this gap. When I was about 14, I wasn't really ready to move up to adult books so I just stopped reading.'

4 It's a gap that publishers have been keen to fill with a massive expansion of books aimed at teenagers. 'It's exciting because teenagers can now read all sorts of things, from soggy growing-up stuff to some really extraordinary storytelling,' says Wendy Cooling, an expert on children's literature and a judge for the new Book Trust Prize for teenage books. But Cross feels that these books have a basic image problem. 'The covers are usually bright and garish, the size of the text, the whole image of these books puts you down because they look like kids' books even though the subject matter might be quite adult in nature.'

5 So what can parents do to keep teenagers reading? Cross read factual books when he couldn't find the right fiction. 'Get them adult books on anything they're really interested in. For me it was scuba diving.' Cooling believes we need to be more relaxed about teenagers' reading. 'We expect them to go for something harder than we might go for ourselves. Adults read all sorts of things, from football magazines to blockbusters, yet we expect much more of them. Parents often dismiss what their teenagers read as rubbish when it just isn't to their taste.'

6 Bookshops are like warehouses and even an adult can find just choosing a book difficult and daunting. 'Go into a bookshop – not necessarily to buy anything, but just to browse together and talk about books,' Cooling suggests. Find out what they are reading at school – and don't buy them more of the same. She bought her niece one such sequel and 'she threw it back at me; the last thing she wanted was another one. Reading for pleasure is what matters most, so that can mean anything from short stories to graphic novels.'

7 My children know they can always sting me for money for a book if for nothing else. Every Christmas they each receive a stack of paperbacks wrapped individually in different coloured tissue paper and tied together with ribbon. Half never get read but they all get thumbed through and it's the smell and feel of books as ever-present objects that counts. Last year, in a pointless effort at economising, I said they would each only get one big present. 'And our book stack,' replied the teenager firmly, who then gave me a list of what she wanted. How could I deny them that?

QUESTIONS

The following questions are testing your grasp of AF2 and AF4.

The following questions test AF2 – your ability to select and retrieve information from across the whole text.

1. Re-read paragraph 2. Give two reasons that the author gives for teenagers not wanting to read.

2. Find one word or phrase from paragraph 2 that expresses just how difficult it can be for teenagers to find time for reading.

3. Explain the two further reasons for teenagers not reading that Chris Cross gives in paragraphs 3 and 4.

4. What do paragraphs 5 and 6 suggest about the ways that parents can help their teenagers to keep reading?

The following questions test AF4 – your ability to discuss the way a text is structured and organised.

1. What is the purpose of having paragraph 3, which contains Chris Cooling's personal account of why he stopped reading, before paragraph 4?

2. Why do you think the writer opens paragraph 6 with the sentence: 'Bookshops are like warehouses and even an adult can find just choosing a book difficult and daunting.'

3. Why does the author start and end her piece with personal anecdotes?

VOLUNTEERING
– THE NEW SERVICE

Welcome to the new look for the former Service Section! We've changed the name and made the volunteering section more flexible in line with today's huge range of exciting volunteering possibilities, great news for everyone!

After consulting with large numbers of young people and Leaders, we're sure you'll all be as excited as we are about the difference this will make.

Why we've changed the name

Talking to young people, it was clear that the word 'service' was a little out of date and often misleading. They linked the word to things like punishment using community service and silver service waiters! 'Volunteering', on the other hand, explains exactly what's involved and is used throughout the UK to describe giving up your time to help others. We still appreciate the positive connotations of the word service, and so we have kept the sectional aim the same: 'to encourage service to individuals and to the community'.

What can young people do?

There's a vast choice of possible volunteering that young people can take part in, in today's communities. We wanted to add clarity to the section by making it easier and so we have five different categories for young people to choose from.

- **Helping people** – Direct contact with people e.g. youth groups, day centres for older people or being a young carer.
- **Working in the environment or with animals** – Hands-on work e.g. canal conservation, litter picking or helping at an animal shelter.
- **Helping a charity or community organisation** – Supporting their work e.g. fundraising, online administration or hospital radio.
- **Community Action/Awareness** – Getting your voice heard e.g. school council, anti-racism campaign or working with the police against anti-social behaviour.
- **Teaching, Coaching or Leadership** – Passing knowledge onto others e.g. sports coaching, teaching singing or supporting literacy classes

Every type of volunteering that a young person might want to do should fit in to at least one. We want to encourage participants to create their own programme to meet the needs of their community, to support a cause they're passionate about or to help people they're concerned about.

Practical volunteering

We believe that volunteering should be about getting out there and making a real difference. It is great to hear about all the amazing ways that young people are having an impact as part of their DofE programmes. We know that some young people, however, are learning skills that might be used to benefit the community in the future, but aren't actually taking part in practical volunteering.

Training courses, such as first aid, lifesaving awards, police and fire services are sometimes being used to complete the Volunteering section, with no actual volunteering taking place. Sometimes young people haven't always chosen the activity and can feel unmotivated by it, which is in contrast to the principles for the Volunteering section.

So how can these courses be used? Learning these skills is still extremely important and, if young people want to take part in these training programmes, we would encourage you to suggest that they be used for the Skills section. Young people can then put these skills into practice for their next level of DofE programme.

Alternatively, you could encourage the local organiser of these courses to change the content so that there is at least three-quarters practical volunteering. There are many opportunities to turn police and fire courses into practical volunteering in the Community Awareness category, look out for ideas on our website.

Team volunteering

We know that many young people are already volunteering in teams, but we're really encouraging more young people to volunteer in this way. This is because young people tell us how much they enjoy volunteering with other people their age and they also recognise the different skills you can gain from working in a group. We want to promote the many, excellent existing team volunteering opportunities that are on offer, but we also want to encourage young people to create their own.

If you have any great examples of youth-led and/or team volunteering opportunities, or any questions about the new section then please contact **volunteering@DofE.org**

Practical volunteering example:

Gemma, Silver DofE participant, Secondary School
As part of their Bronze DofE programme a number of young people trained for their Lifesaving Bronze Medallion award for their Skills section. One young person decided to put these skills into practice for the Volunteering section of her Silver DofE programme. Gemma decided to help the school swimming club offer free, after-school swimming lessons to more young people and volunteered her time to help supervise the pool alongside a fully qualified pool lifeguard. She was really pleased that because of the skills she had learnt to achieve her Bronze Award, she was able to make a difference in her school community.

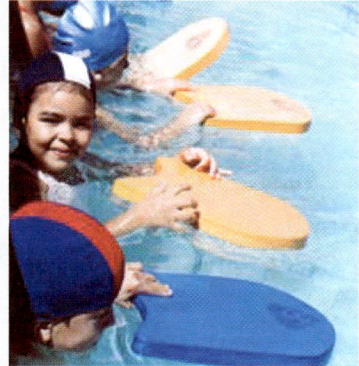

Team volunteering example:

Bronze DofE group, Young Offender Institute
A group of Bronze participants in a YOI decided to plan, set up and run a charity football event to raise money for charity. They had meetings where they allocated roles to each young person, depending on their interests and skills, e.g. advertising, arranging the time and place, recruiting the football teams, organising the match and refereeing. All of the young people made joint decisions on major things and the charity that they were going to raise money for. They researched the charity in detail so they could understand where the money was going, as well as be able to tell others about the cause. The team of young volunteers held sessions after the event to work out how they would get the money to the charity as well as to evaluate their own performance over the three months, as individuals and as part of the team.

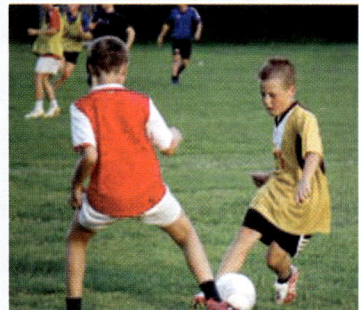

QUESTIONS

The following questions are testing your grasp of AF2 and AF3.

The following questions test AF2 – your ability to select and retrieve information from across the whole text.

1. Look at paragraph one.
Why has the Duke of Edinburgh scheme stopped using the word 'service'?
Why have they started using the word 'volunteering'?

2. What five categories of volunteering are available to young people through the scheme?

3. What are the main benefits of team volunteering expressed towards the end of this article?

4. Re-read the 'Practical volunteering example'. How did Gemma benefit from the experience she gained during her Bronze award?

The following questions test AF3 – your ability to infer and interpret information and ideas from texts.

1. What does the writer mean when they write: 'Volunteering should be about getting out there and making a real difference.'?

2. What point is the writer trying to make when they write: 'Sometimes young people haven't always chosen the activity and can feel unmotivated…' ?

3. How does the writer express a positive attitude towards volunteering in this article? You may wish to consider:

   • the facts given about volunteers' experiences
   • the language used in the article.

Briefing

Do cell phones cause cancer?

A prominent cancer research institute last week warned faculty and staff to limit their use of mobile phones because of the possible risk of cancer. Should cell phone users be worried?

Are cell phones dangerous?

The scientific consensus has long been that they are not – though recently, some troubling research has led to new doubts.

As soon as mobile phones began hitting the market in the 1980s, concerns were raised that the electromagnetic radio waves they emit might cause brain tumours and other types of cancer. But as cell phones became ubiquitous, at least a dozen major studies found no such link. The Food and Drug Administration said recently that three large epidemiological studies since 2000 showed 'no harmful effects' from cell phone use, and the World Health Organization holds a similar view. The theory that cell phones pose health risks, says Dr Eugene Flamm, chairman of neurosurgery at New York's Montefiore Medical Center, 'defies credulity.'

What's the basis of that contention?

Cell phones emit non-ionising radiation, waves of energy that are too weak to break the chemical bonds within cells or to cause the DNA damage known to cause cancer. There is simply no known biological mechanism to explain how non-ionising radiation might lead to cancer. But some researchers say that the lack of a known mechanism does not rule out the possibility that one exists and has yet to be understood. They also say that older studies on cell phone safety contained a major flaw.

What's the flaw?

As the FDA itself acknowledges, most of the studies examined cell phone use over a period of about three years – not long enough to rule out the possibility of *long-term* effects. 'It takes at least 10, 20 or 30 years to see exposure to cancer,' says Israeli neuroscientist Dr Siegal Sadetzki. She points out that it took decades before scientists could prove that people exposed to radiation at Hiroshima had a much higher incidence of brain tumours. Critics also say that the studies have largely ignored the impact of cell phones on teenagers and preteens, whose developing brains may be more vulnerable, especially since many of them tend to use cell phones for hours every day.

What does recent research show?

Two major studies have found an *association*, though not a *causal* relationship, between cell phone use and certain cancers. Last year, the *American Journal of Epidemiology* published data from Israel finding a 50 per cent higher risk of cancer of the parotid, a salivary gland near the ear, among habitual cell phone users. A Swedish analysis of 16 studies in the journal *Occupational and Environmental Medicine* showed a doubling of risk for acoustic neuroma, a tumour that occurs where the ear meets the brain, after 10 years of heavy cell phone use. 'There are some very disconcerting findings that suggest a problem,' says Dr Louis Selsin, editor of *Microwave News*, an industry publication that tracks the research, 'although it's much too early to reach a conclusive view.'

What does the industry say?

Citing the authority of the World Health Organization, cell phone companies say the technology poses no known risks and requires no precautions. They also stress that radiation levels from cell phones fall well within government safety guidelines. 'The overwhelming majority of studies that have been published in scientific journals around the globe show that wireless phones do not pose a health risk,' says a spokesman for the Wireless Association, the leading industry trade group. But cell phone makers and service providers are nervously awaiting the results of an ambitious international research effort, called Interphone, on the health impact of cell phone use being conducted by WHO's International Agency for Research on Cancer. The study, culling and analysing data spanning more than a decade from 13 countries, is expected to be published later this year.

Any early word on what it will conclude?

Many experts say it will raise new red flags. They're basing that expectation on the fact that some of the countries involved in the study, including Israel and Sweden, have already gone public with their own results. A recent analysis by Swedish oncologist Dr Lennart Hardell looked at 10 European studies published between 2001 and 2007, most of which will also be part of the Interphone study. Hardell found 'a consistent pattern of association' between certain brain tumours and long-term cell phone use. A 2007 research paper in Finland looked at brain cancer studies in five North European countries and found a 'significantly increased' risk after cell phone use of more than 10 years.

So what should consumers do?

Nobody is saying we should all throw away our cell phones. But many health experts have stepped forward in recent months to say they now have enough concern that they are advising users to take some precautions – such as using speaker mode or earpieces, rather than holding the phone directly to your head. Just last week, the director of the prestigious University of Pittsburgh Cancer Institute, Dr Ronald Herberman, warned his faculty and staff to limit cell phone use because of the possible cancer risk. Herberman cited a 'growing body of literature' – including unpublished studies – that link long-term cell phone use to adverse health effects, though he acknowledged the findings are far from conclusive. 'We shouldn't wait for a definitive study to come out,' Herberman said, 'but err on the side of being safe rather than sorry later.'

Worrying about the kids

Advocates who worry about cell phones' impact on human health say they're most concerned about children, who face a lifetime of exposure. 'They may be much more affected,' says Dr Paul Rosch of New York Medical College. 'Their brains are growing rapidly, and their skulls are thinner.' Some researchers are now advising that pending further study, children should use land lines to speak to friends, and use cell phones only in emergencies. Dr Siegal Sadetzki, the Israeli researcher, says it's reasonable to assume that whatever harmful effects cell phones produce 'will accumulate,' so children are particularly at risk. That doesn't mean banning cell phones, she says, but finding ways to reduce radiation exposure among users. 'Nobody will stop using this technology. There are car accidents and still we keep driving cars,' she says. 'The question is, what precautions do we take?'

From *The Week*, August 2008.

QUESTIONS

The following questions are testing your grasp of AF4 and AF6.

The following questions test AF4 – your ability to discuss the way a text is structured and organised.

1 This article uses subheadings to divide up the material. Why do you think the writer chose to place the section headed 'Are cell phones dangerous?' at the beginning of the article?

2 Choose two other sections of the article. Why do you think they have been placed where they are in the article? Explain your views.

3 Look at the text box – titled 'Worrying about the kids'. The content of this paragraph can be summed up by the statements below. Place them in the correct order to represent the content of the box in the correct order.

- It gives some contrary advice.
- It explains why children are possibly more affected than others.
- The article names the main concern of those worried about cell phones.
- It gives advice on cell phone use for children.

4 Looking again at the text box titled 'Worrying about the kids', what is the reason behind putting the two doctors' comments in the order that has been used (Dr Paul Rosch first and then Dr Siegal Sadetzki)?

5 The passage uses italics in two different ways. Explain each use.

6 Consider the five dashes used in the passage. What is their purpose?

The following questions test AF6 – your ability to work out the viewpoint, attitudes and purpose shown in a text.

1 Which of the following statements most closely reflects the overall attitude shown by this article?

- This article is totally negative about cell phones.
- This article suggests that fears about cell phones and health are unfounded.
- This article suggests that we should be less complacent about the dangers of cell phones.
- The article suggests that we should not make up our mind about cell phones until the results of long-term studies come in.

2 How does this article suggest that cell phones may be dangerous for our health? You may wish to consider:

- the way the writer uses research data and statistics
- the way the writer uses quotations from experts
- the way the writer organises the article
- the language used by the writer.

Jeffrey's Bay

1. J-Bay, known to surfers world wide as a strip of geographic jewellery, has also been spoken of as SA's most valuable liquid asset. Any surfer (or anyone for that matter) who has had the privilege of viewing first-hand those long, perfect lines, will all too well comprehend the metaphorical significance of those words.

2. The Sixties, the year of the real soul surfers and the introduction of the short surfboard, saw very little change in the town. The surfers arrived, did their thing and departed, like ghosts in the night. They were, in essence, the pioneers of the J-Bay surfing experience, their involvement and presence the synthesis of the existing soul and character of the town.

3. All the while the long perfect lines rolled in from Supers through Tubes and finally to the Point. In '68, almost 10 years after the discovery of J-Bay, it happened. Two surfers dared to take on Supers.

4. Imagine, for a moment, how you'd feel confronting a hitherto feared Island wave… a wall of water stretching menacingly forever down the line… then, just before you take off on the first ever ride of this unchallenged break, your eyes take in an expanse of rock snatching at the pounding curtain… Gulp… Perhaps this is how it felt to those first two Supers pioneers, two Aussies known only as Morrie and the Beast, who, late one evening, rode the pumping break – wearing tackles to protect their feet from the jagged rocks.

5. Enter the Seventies. The introduction to the surf leash and the decade of the first really deep tube-riding. The decade of change, new music and, above all else, new attitudes, all contrasting with those of the Sixties.

6. J-Bay was not without change during those times. The first local surfers put down roots in town. Surfboards were now being shaped locally, all with an eye to conquering 'The Bay'. Many of the locals who have developed a deep-rooted passion for the town would like to see the Point area through to the main beach declared a Nature Reserve. As Cheron says, 'It's a charming little Afrikaans fishing village which can evolve but its beauty and character must be retained.'

7. Although to many the peeling perfection of Supers remains J-Bay, to the locals and many others there is much more to the town. Larry Levin says it all. 'If I had to start all over again, I would do it all here. I'm not a city boy, and no matter what the development, J-Bay is the country.'

8. Those words, echoing across the tubular expanse of the globe, reverberate with the everlasting indescribable thrill, stoke, call it what you like, that every surfer experiences as he stands on the rocks, waiting for the lull, about to paddle into one of the wonders of the world, Supertubes at J-Bay.

9. Yes, even with the expanding commercial development of the town, J-Bay is still what it was in the Sixties: a town of surf and soul.

Adapted from an article in *Zigzag*.

QUESTIONS

The following questions are testing your grasp of AF5.

The following questions test AF5 – your ability to understand the effect of language used in a text.

1 Select two words from paragraph 1 that suggest that the writer feels positively about Jeffrey's Bay (J-Bay).

2 a)   What does the phrase 'geographical jewellery' suggest?
   b)   What does the phrase 'liquid asset' suggest?

3 The writer tells us that when surfing first started in Jeffrey's Bay the town 'saw very little change'. Select two other phrases from paragraph 2 which suggest that the surfing did not make much difference to the town when it first started.

4 How does the way that paragraph 3 is written suggest that one of the biggest waves that regularly forms at Jeffrey's Bay, called 'Supers', was a difficult wave to surf?

5 Re-read paragraph 4. How does the writer convey the danger that the first surfers faced when they decided to surf 'Supers'?
You may wish to consider:

   • the way other surfers felt about the wave
   • the language used to describe the land around the bay
   • the use of language to describe the sea.

6 What does the phrase 'put down roots in town' (paragraph 6) suggest about the surfers?

7 What does the use of 'peeling' (paragraph 7) as an adjective to describe a wave suggest about the water and how it moves/looks?

8 How does the writer express the extreme emotions that they and other people feel about Jeffrey's Bay? (You may use examples from the whole article.)

Harry Potter 'is too boring and grown-up for young readers'

> ➢ **Children's laureate attacks the boy wizard**
> ➢ **I would not read them to my children, he says**

(1) They may have sold more than 350 million copies in 65 countries around the world, but J. K. Rowling's Harry Potter books are boring and inappropriate for young readers, according to the Children's Laureate.

(2) Michael Rosen, 62, the poet and author of *We're Going on a Bear Hunt*, succeeded Jacqueline Wilson as the fifth children's laureate in June. A £10,000 bursary goes with the post, which involves promoting reading and writing for children.

(3) Despite their popularity, however, it seems that Rosen is not a fan of the boy wizard books that have earned Rowling an estimated £560 million and spurred young readers into queueing up for copies.

(4) 'They don't grab me personally,' he said. The narratives are complex and most young children would struggle to cope with their challenging and often sinister themes. He would not choose to read them to his own children, he said, because he did not want to bore them.

(5) 'I am distant from them whereas I read some kids' books and I get quite drawn in emotionally to them,' Rosen said. 'Whereas authors like Enid Blyton are hand-holding narrators who lead children into safe environments, J. K. Rowling is more of an adult writer in that she leaves you hanging in the air at the end of chapters with no idea what is going to happen next.'

(6) 'Figures appear and you don't know whether they are a goodie or a baddie. You would think, traditionally, "That is for an older reader", because young children more often than not cannot cope with that. My seven-year-old daughter watches the films, but they tend to spell it out a bit more. I have not read the books to her; you do not want to bore your kids.'

(7) Rosen is not one for avoiding controversy. He began his two-year term as Children's Laureate by attacking pupil testing, saying that it was destroying poetry, and also criticised the reading method synthetic phonics, a literacy scheme that was trialled in schools in Scotland and has been praised widely. Its supporters include Gordon Brown.

(8) The Harry Potter books have given rise to a £7 billion film and merchandising industry. The seven-book series began with *Harry Potter and the Philosopher's Stone*, which was published in June 1997. The final book, *Harry Potter and the Deathly Hallows*, broke all records when it was released last July, selling 11 million copies in Britain and America within 24 hours.

(9) Speaking during a tour of Scotland to promote reading among school pupils, Rosen said that the Harry Potter books deserved credit for encouraging a generation of children to read, but he feared that their success might prevent young people from discovering other authors.

(10) Julie Bertagna, an award-winning children's author from Glasgow, who is also among a group of children's reading champions appointed by the Scottish Parliament, said that she suspected that some parents had been forcing the books on children before they were ready to read them. 'If they were too young it could hinder them, but if they meet them at the right age they can learn to handle big books with lots of characters and complex worlds, such as those written by Philip Pullman,' she added.

(11) Shami Chakrabarti, the director of the human rights group Liberty and chairwoman of the panel of judges that chose Rosen as the Children's Laureate, said that the books encompassed universal themes, making them ideal reading for all age groups. 'Racism, the challenges of diversity and the dilemmas of the War on Terror are all to be found lurking within the magical world of Harry Potter,' she said.

(12) Randall Stevenson, Professor of English Literature at the University of Edinburgh, added: 'They are not exactly *The Lord of the Rings* but I think they deserve their success.'

From *The Times*, May 2008

QUESTIONS

The following questions are testing your grasp of AF6 and AF4.

The following questions test AF6 – your ability to work out the viewpoint, attitudes and purpose shown in a text.

1   Complete the following assessment of each paragraph of the article, summing up whether you feel the paragraph was positive or negative about the Harry Potter books overall.

Paragraph	Positive	Negative	Neutral	Mixed
1				
2				
3				
4				
5				
6				
7				
8				
9				
10				
11				
12				

2   What are Rosen's main criticisms of the Potter series? Use the whole article as the basis of your answer.

3   Does Julie Bertagna agree with Rosen?

4   Does Shami Chakrabarti agree with Rosen?

The following questions test AF4 – your ability to discuss the way a text is structured and organised.

1   Paragraph 3 combines the fact that Rosen 'is not a fan' with information about the book's popularity. Why do you think the author creates this contrast?

2   Why do you think that the writer included the information about Rosen's other 'controversial' criticisms in this article (paragraph 7)?

3   Why does the journalist include the facts and figures about Harry Potter book sales in paragraph 8 rather than earlier or later in the article?

4   Why does the author include factual information about Julie Bertagna before her point of view is quoted (paragraph 10)?

5   Why do you think that the article ends with the quote from Professor Stevenson?

The 'helicopter parents' hovering over their adult children

Children used to be more or less left to their own devices by their parents once they had finished school. But the trend is for ever-increasing hands-on parental involvement, not just through university but even into the workplace. Kate Hilpern reports

1 Once upon a time – not so long ago, actually – the university admissions service, Ucas, was considered by many to hold the golden ticket to adulthood. Having selected your university choices, you'd sit tight and wait for the offers – offers that you knew would change the course of your life and cut those apron strings with a pleasing snip.

2 How things have changed. This year, parents were granted a licence to manage their offspring's university application for the first time. One in ten of half a million university applicants ticked a new box on the form that enables them to name a parent or guardian as their agent, allowing parents to act on their children's behalf in the fight to get a place at university. 'Your experience of form-filling will be invaluable to your child!' boasts the Ucas website. Welcome to the age of helicopter parenting, so named because these mothers and fathers hover closely overhead, rarely out of reach, whether their children need them or not.

3 It's not just a question of parents helping their child get a place at university. Even after arriving, students are increasingly found to be phoning mum and dad during lectures and asking them to attend open days and careers fairs. Such is the trend that Huddersfield University has set up a 'family liaison officer' to feed information to parents round-the-clock about their kids' progress. Nor does it stop with graduation. One major accounting firm reports that it has had mothers pretending to be their graduate children's secretaries to find out more about the job they're applying for and, at Hewlett-Packard, parents have gone as far as trying to negotiate their son's or daughter's salary or relocation package.

4 The mobile phone has been described as the 'world's longest umbilical cord', and no wonder. Modern parents admit to calling their offspring several times a day well into their twenties. They are so used to being able to communicate with them 24/7 (not to mention chauffeuring them to every 'enrichment activity', taking on their school projects, bad-mouthing teachers who tell them off) that they think nothing of making calls not just to, but also on behalf of adult children. 'I want to make sure you don't offer my daughter an overdraft, as she doesn't deal well with debt'; 'My son won't be coming into work today, he's got a cold'; 'My daughter always travels first-class. Is she really expected to travel second-class on business?" are all genuine examples.

5 Far from begging mum and dad to please, please give it up, many over-18s seem to welcome such indulgence. In one case, a new recruit to a transport company was overheard on the phone to his mother, saying: 'I have got to go to London tomorrow and they haven't even told me how to get there.' 'The employer threw up her hands in anger and frustration – here was someone working for a transport company, was 21 and had spent three years at university who was aggrieved because he hadn't been given a detailed map,' says Carl Gilleard, chief executive the Association of Graduate Recruiters (AGR), who reports that such examples are not rare.

6 Sue Beck makes no apology for offering to attend job interviews with her 25-year-old daughter, and sees no irony in offering the explanation that children are 'slower to grow up these days'. "Sometimes she'll ask me to do things like call the doctor to say she'll be late, and until recently, there were a few times when she wanted me to phone her work to say she'd be late or that she was ill. I'm happy to help. Why not?"

7 Bank managers, universities, employers, landlords and the rest of society, could, of course, tell these parents and their offspring to get a grip. But what is actually happening, as Ucas illustrates, is quite the opposite. With many universities seeing parental interest as an inevitable consequence of imposing tuition fees, Newcastle Business School is by no means exceptional in its decision to run special sessions for parents. 'In the past, parents wouldn't typically come to university open days, but in the past three years it has become the norm,' says Tim Nichol, associate dean for undergraduate programmes. 'We felt the only way round it was to start running two sessions – one for the students and one for the parents, who seem to be particularly interested in the Ucas application system, as well as the finances, accommodation and even meeting the academics.'

8 Intrigued by just how much influence parents have over their offspring's decision, Nichol carried out a survey. 'We found that 80% say their parents have a lot or some influence.' Just 2% said they had none at all – a far cry from my own experience in the 1980s, when my friends and I would rather have given up drinking for a year than ask our parents where we should go to university. Most of us knew the answer already – as far away as possible – whereas a growing number of today's undergraduates are studying at the university nearest to their family.

From *The Week*, September 2008

QUESTIONS

The following questions are testing your grasp of AF3.

The following questions test AF3 – your ability to infer and interpret information and ideas from texts.

1 Paragraph 1 suggests that teenagers used to want to break away and be independent from their parents when they left home for university. Explain how the following phrases suggest this:

a) '… the golden ticket to adulthood.'

b) '…cut those apron strings with a pleasing snip.'

2 The language used in paragraph 3 suggests that the writer feels that things are getting a little 'over the top'. Explain where and how this idea is expressed.

3 What is meant by the metaphor 'The mobile phone has been described as the "world's longest umbilical cord"' (paragraph 4)?

4 What can you infer from the writer's use of the words 'admit to' in paragraph 4 and 'indulgence' in paragraph 5?

5 How is Sue Beck feeling when she asks 'Why not?' in paragraph 6?

6 What do you infer from the fact that a growing number of undergraduates are studying at the university nearest their family (paragraph 8)?

Flight

1   Cries of '*Khawulele! Wenk'umntu!*' shattered the stillness of the saucer-like
village nestling in the valley, surrounded by green hills and scrub-dotted
mountains.

Echoes bounced from the hilltops, clashed mid-air, ricocheted and fell in
5   jumbled noises that boomed, invading our ears and jamming out all other
sounds.

weh weh weh khauu khauu khauu
leh leh leh leh tuu tuu tuu!

Like a powerful magnet, the commotion pulled us away from the rag dolls
10 that had so occupied us but a moment before.

Iii-iiiWuu-uuuuu!
Mmbaa – mbeeehh-ni!
Qhaaa-wuu-lee-laani!

An old man: short, tight-curled springs of wool on his head making a greyish-
15 white skull cap tottered past in what I saw as his earnest attempt at running.
His left hand clasped the blanket loosely wrapped around his body; his right
arm, from the shoulder, was stuck out as if from a toga. Thin, long, and bony,
it swung back and front each time to his intended accelerated step. Held
high in the hand, the *knobkerrie* jutted out and away from his body. Each time
20 he shouted – '*Mbambeni!* – Catch her!' he stretched out the arm holding the
knobkerrie, pointing the stick toward the mountain.

My eyes leapt to where he pointed. The mountain was playing a game
of hide and seek with the sun. Or was it with the clouds? Anyway, half the
mountain had disappeared. I threw my eyes towards the remaining half.
25 There, distance-shrunk figures scurried, hurried, ran and scrambled.

Ahead, a lone figure darted like a hare with a pack of dogs hard on its
tail. The clouds were no idle players, I saw. They were the third party to this
game; and they would make the telling difference.

Clearly, that day, witnessed the birth of tears. The clouds wept and
30 showered soft tears of mist onto the silent mountain. Would the fleeing figure
gain the mist blanket in time? The sun smiled and the mist disappeared in a
spray of long, hot, yellow needles, the children of the sun.

There she was, clearly, I saw her. Surely, her pursuers too could see her? –
see her as I did?
35 My insides churned. A hot ball of fear curled inside my stomach. But the
clouds, not to be outdone, wept. Thick, fat, dark-grey spears fell. Fast and
hard they came. Thick, fat; safe for her to be enveloped in and lost to her
pursuers.

'*Uye phi? Uye phi?* Where's she gone?'

40 Sounds of distress from those who were bent on her capture reached me. I held my breath as I strained with her, willing her to elude them, urging her on and on and on.

My last glimpse of her: blue German-print dress paled to a soft sky-blue by distance and lack of light … there she was, flitting here and there between
45 boulders, her long new-wife-length dress making her seem without feet. As she hurried escaping, she appeared to me to be riding the air – no part of her body making contact with the ground.

Away she floated; the men plodded behind her.

I saw her waft into the wall of mist. I saw it close the crack she'd almost
50 made gliding into it. Like a fish slicing into water, she'd but disturbed it. And it rearranged itself, accepting her into itself. And away from those who harried her.

I cannot remember her face at all. It was a long time ago and perhaps she had not tarried long with us. I don't know. But I remember her leaving. And
55 that is because it taught me about determination, the power of one's will.

She was a young woman, a new wife. Her husband, my uncle, was away at work in one of the mines where all the men of the village went for a very long time. Later, much later, with great learning to aid me order my world, I would come to know the precise length of their stay – eleven months each
60 year. However, this knowledge was light years away from me that fear-filled day long, long ago.

It must have been midday for the sun was well up and we children were already outside at play; that is, those of us too little to go to the one mud-walled, grass-thatched house called school.
65 I know I should've been sad at losing an aunt. I know that she was a good *makoti*, cooked and cleaned well, and we children were saved from a lot of chores by her coming – new wives are worked like donkeys as initiation into her new status. I know I should have sympathised with my uncle who lost not only a wife but also cattle, the *lobola*, he had given for her.
70 All I know, is the thrill I felt watching her escape into the thick grey cloud and mist.

By Sindiwe Magona

Khawulele! Wenk'umntu!: Stop her! Everyone!

knobkerrie: a small knob stick

Mbambeni!: Catch her!

Uye phi?: Where has she gone?

makoti: new bride

lobola: bride price

QUESTIONS

The following questions are testing your grasp of AF3 and AF5.

The following questions test AF3 – your ability to infer and interpret information and ideas from texts.

1 Pick out two phrases that suggest the village is in a valley.

2 How do lines 4–6 suggest that the cries heard were very loud?

3 What leads you to think that the narrator was a child at the time when the described event took place?

4 How does the narrator feel about the runaway both at the time and later when he or she reflects on it as an adult? Explain what makes you feel this way. You may wish to consider:
- the way the narrator describes the woman
- the words that the narrator uses to describe the pursuers
- the information the narrator later learns about the life of a new wife.

5 Why might the young woman have run away from her new home? Support your answer with references from the story.

The following questions test AF5 – your ability to understand the effect of language used in a text.

1 What is the effect of the following phrases:
   a) 'like a powerful magnet' (line 9)
   b) 'like a hare with a pack of dogs hard on its tail' (line 26)
   c) 'Like a fish slicing into water' (line 50)?

2 How is a sense of urgency created in lines 22–28?

3 How does the writer use the weather in lines 29–38?

I know why the caged bird sings

A free bird leaps
on the back of the wind
and floats downstream
till the current ends
and dips his wings
in the orange sun rays
and dares to claim the sky.

But a bird that stalks
down his narrow cage
can seldom see through
his bars of rage
his wings are clipped and
his feet are tied
so he opens his throat to sing.

The caged bird sings
with fearful trill
of the things unknown
but longed for still
and his tune is heard
on the distant hill
for the caged bird
sings of freedom.

The free bird thinks of another breeze
and the trade winds soft through the sighing trees
and the fat worms waiting on a dawn-bright lawn
and he names the sky his own.

But a caged bird stands on the grave of dreams
his shadow shouts on a nightmare scream
his wings are clipped and his feet are tied
so he opens his throat to sing.

The caged bird sings
with a fearful trill
of things unknown
but longed for still
and his tune is heard
on the distant hill
for the caged bird
sings of freedom.

By *Maya Angelou*

QUESTIONS

The following questions are testing your grasp of AF5 and AF6.

The following questions test AF5 – your ability to understand the effect of language used in a text.

1 Explain how these two quotations suggest what life is like for the birds in the poem.

Verse	Quotation	Effect of the quotation
1	'and floats downstream till the current ends'	
2	'Stalks down his narrow cage'	

2 Make a list of four verbs used to describe the free bird and explain the effect that they have on the reader.

3 Make a list of three verbs used to describe the caged bird and explain the effect that they have on the reader.

4 What is the effect of the phrase 'dares to claim' on our understanding of the bird's attitude towards the sky?

5 The birds in this poem could be seen as a metaphor. What could they represent? What does the caged bird's song represent?

The following questions test AF6 – your ability to work out the viewpoint, attitudes and purpose shown in a text.

1 Select a word or phrase that suggests that Angelou believes imprisoning creatures is wrong.

2 Verse 1 and verse 4 end with a similar line: the thoughts of the caged bird: 'and dares to claim the sky' (verse 1), 'and he names the sky his own' (verse 4). What is Angelou suggesting about the way imprisonment affects the bird's attitudes?

3 Re-read verse 2. Angelou suggests that the fact that the bird cannot fly freely makes it sing instead. If the bird is a metaphor for mankind, what is she suggesting?

4 What does Angelou think about imprisoning living things? You may wish to refer to:
- the way she describes life in prison
- the way she describes the life of a free creature
- what she says about how being imprisoned affects the ambitions of prisoners.

Flowers for Algernon is a novel by Daniel Keyes. Charlie is an adult with learning difficulties who would love to be able to read and write. After an experimental operation his dreams come true – but the changes to his life are not what he, or the scientists, had expected. This extract is from the adaptation by Bert Coules. It shows how Charlie's life has changed since his operation.

SCENE 20	*Int: Another room.*

BERT *the technician sorts out his cards, as before.*

BERT OK, Charlie, here we go.

CHARLIE It's the inkblot test!

BERT Sorry?

CHARLIE The cards with the inkblots on them. I took this test before. Before the operation.

BERT Ah, you remember, do you?

CHARLIE (*angrily*): Of course I remember.

BERT Yes, of course. Sorry.

CHARLIE Right.

BERT OK. Now, I want you to look at this first card . . .

He lays a card on the table.

What might this be? People see all sorts of things in these inkblots. Tell me what it might be for you. What does it make you think of?

CHARLIE (*amazed*): What did you say?

BERT What does it make you think of?

CHARLIE You mean there are no pictures hidden in those inkblots?

BERT What?

CHARLIE Pictures. Hidden in the inkblots. Last time you told me that everyone could see them and you wanted me to find them too.

BERT Charlie, last time I used almost exactly the same words I used just now. I always say the same thing.

CHARLIE I don't believe you.

BERT Why should I lie?

CHARLIE To make fun of me.

BERT Charlie!

CHARLIE I was sure . . .

CHARLIE *is very uncertain. He pulls himself together.*

Show me that card.

He slides it towards himself.

It looks like a pair of bats hanging upside down.

Next.

BERT *puts down another.*

Two men fencing. Next.

The speed builds.

A clown's face. A vase of flowers. A lion. A butterfly with an injured wing. Wait.

BERT What?

CHARLIE How can you be sure I'm not just saying anything at random? How do you know I'm not making a fool of you?

Out.

CHARLIE (*tape*): I went back to the factory. I figured out a new way to line up the machines on the production line, and I overheard Mr Donnegan the owner say it will save thousands of pounds a year in labour and increased production. He gave me a fifty pound bonus. Tomorrow I plan to take Joe and Frank out to lunch to celebrate.

SCENE 21 *Int: The factory floor.*

JOE *and* FRANK *are very uneasy with the new* CHARLIE.

JOE No, sorry, Charlie mate. I've got to do some shopping for the wife. I promised, you know?

FRANK Yeah, and I'm meeting my cousin for lunch.

Arranged it weeks ago. Bleeding shame.

JOE Yeah. (*Escaping*) Sorry.

FRANK (*going*): Yeah. . .

A moment. CHARLIE *sighs, dunks his mop in its bucket and drains it off.*

Out.

CHARLIE (*tape*): It's almost as if they're afraid of me. Hardly anybody talks to me, or jokes around the way they used to. It makes the job sort of lonely. I'm going to try to get up the nerve to ask Miss Kinnian to have dinner with me to celebrate my bonus. I'll ask her tonight at the hospital.

SCENE 22 *Int*: **DR STRAUSS'** *room.*

A fierce argument is in progress.

DR NEMUR For God's sake, Strauss! It's my experiment and my research, and I'll publish the results whenever I think fit.

DR STRAUSS Your experiment? Who performed the operation? Whose techniques made the whole thing possible? Who found him, for God's sake?

DR NEMUR Joint names then, I'll grant you that.

DR STRAUSS Oh, thank you very much.

DR NEMUR But we publish at the end of this month.

DR STRAUSS	It's too soon! We're still not one hundred percent sure.
DR NEMUR	Too soon. If we wait any longer, word will get out anyway.
DR STRAUSS	And spoil your thunder!

As the argument continues, we cut to:

SCENE 23	*Int: Outside the door*

Very close, CHARLIE *is listening to the muffled voices. We hear him wincing at the ferocity of the row.*

DR NEMUR	What do you mean by that?
DR STRAUSS	You're more interested in your own glory than you are in the experiment. Charlie means nothing to you.
DR NEMUR	My glory! What about you? You're just trying to ride to fame on my work.
DR STRAUSS	Your work would mean nothing without my breakthrough in neurosurgery.
DR NEMUR	Breakthrough! You flatter yourself, doctor . . .

But all this has been going on behind:

| MISS K | (*Off*) Charlie? |

CHARLIE *jumps.*

CHARLIE	Miss Kinnian.
MISS K	(*approaching*): Why are you waiting out here?
CHARLIE	They're arguing again. Come away.

He leads her down the corridor. We go with them. The argument fades.

CHARLIE	They argue all the time now.
MISS K	Yes, I know.
CHARLIE	Miss Kinnian . . .
MISS K	Yes, Charlie?
CHARLIE	I have something to ask you . . .

Out.

| CHARLIE | (*tape*): I don't understand why I never noticed how beautiful Miss Kinnian really is. She has brown eyes and feathery brown hair that comes to the top of her neck. She's only thirty-four! I think from the beginning I had the feeling that she was an unreachable genius – and very, very old. Now, every time I see her she grows younger and more lovely. |

SCENE 24	*Int: A restaurant.*

Quiet and elegant. Very muted music plays.

CHARLIE *pours some wine.*

| CHARLIE | There. |

MISS K Thank you.

They drink. A moment.

You know, Charlie, you'll soon be leaving me behind.

CHARLIE (*laughingly*): Hardly.

MISS K It's true. You're already a better reader than I am. You can take in a whole page at a glance. And you remember every single word you read.

CHARLIE I don't feel intelligent. There are so many things I don't understand.

MISS K You've got to be patient. You're accomplishing in weeks what takes normal people half a lifetime. It's amazing. You're like a giant sponge, soaking things in. Facts, figures, general knowledge. And soon you'll begin to connect them.

CHARLIE Connect them?

MISS K All the different branches of learning are related. They're like steps on a giant ladder that take you up higher and higher to see more and more of the world around you.

CHARLIE That's a wonderful way of putting it.

MISS K I can see only a little bit of the whole, Charlie, and I won't go much higher than I am now – but you'll keep climbing up and up, and see more and more, and each step will open new worlds that you never even knew existed. (*A moment*) I hope . . . I just hope to God –

CHARLIE What?

MISS K I just hope I wasn't wrong, advising you to go into this in the first place.

CHARLIE (*laughingly*): How could you be? It worked, didn't it?

MISS K (*not reassured*): Yes, it worked.

A moment. They look at each other.

CHARLIE I know what you're thinking. No guarantee of permanence. Cheer up. Algernon is still smart, isn't he? And this is only the beginning for me. I know it.

Out.

CHARLIE (*tape*): No guarantee of permanence. I didn't want to think of what that might mean, any more than elderly people want to think about death. But I hadn't lied to her. And I understood what she meant about the levels, because I'd seen some of them already. The thought of leaving her behind made me sad.

I'm in love with Miss Kinnian.

QUESTIONS

The following questions are testing your grasp of AF3

The following questions test AF3 – your ability to infer and interpret information and ideas from texts.

1. What does Bert's reaction to Charlie remembering the inkblot test suggest?

2. How is Charlie's reaction to the test different from his previous reactions to it? What does this suggest about the way that the operation has changed him? Use words and phrases from the extract in your answer.

3. Find one word that expresses how Joe and Frank feel about 'the new Charlie'? Use evidence from scenes 20 and 21 of the extract to explain why they might feel this way.

4. What do scenes 22 and 23 suggest about the two scientists' attitudes towards Charlie and the experiment? You should refer to words and phrases from the extract in your answer.

5. Scene 24 shows us the possibility of further changes in Charlie's life. What are they and how does he feel about them?

   Copy and complete the following chart showing the positive and negative effects of Charlie's improved intelligence.

Quote	Positive effects	Negative effects
'I don't believe you.' 'Why should I lie?' 'To make fun of me.'		
'It's almost as if they're afraid of me.'		
'I think from the beginning … lovely.'		
'There are so many things I don't understand.'		
'… you'll keep climbing up and up and see more and more…'		